Finished Size: Approximately 16″ x 21″

MATERIALS

Bedspread Weight Cotton Thread (size 10),
  approximately 1 ball plus 30 yards
    (282 yards per ball)
Steel crochet hook, size 6 (1.50 mm) **or** size needed
  for gauge

GAUGE: Each Motif = 3″

PATTERN STITCHES

Picot: Ch 3, slip st in stitch just made.

Treble Crochet (abbreviated tr): YO twice, insert hook
in stitch indicated, YO and pull up a loop (4 loops on
hook), (YO and draw through 2 loops on hook) 3 times.

Beginning Shell: Ch 3, (2 dc, ch 3, 3 dc) in same
space.

Shell: (3 Dc, ch 3, 3 dc) in space indicated.

Cluster: ★ YO, insert hook in space indicated and pull
up a loop, YO and draw through 2 loops on hook;
repeat from ★ 2 times **more**, YO and draw through all
4 loops on hook.

Continued on page 3.

FIRST MOTIF

Ch 10, join with slip st to form a ring.

Rnd 1 (Right side): Ch 3, 23 dc in ring; join with slip st to top of beginning ch-3: 24 sts.

Note: Loop a short piece of thread around any stitch to mark last round as **right** side.

Rnd 2: Ch 1, sc in same st and in each dc around; join with slip st to first sc.

Rnd 3: Ch 1, sc in same st and in next sc, work Picot, sc in next sc, (ch 7, skip next sc, sc in next 2 sc, work Picot, sc in next sc) around to last sc, ch 3, tr in first sc to form last loop: 6 loops.

Rnd 4: Ch 3, (2 dc, ch 3, slip st in third ch from hook, 3 dc) in same loop, ★ ch 7, (3 dc, ch 3, slip st in third ch from hook, 3 dc) in next loop; repeat from ★ around, ch 3, tr in top of beginning ch-3 to form last loop.

Rnd 5: Work beginning Shell, ch 11, (work Shell in next loop, ch 11) around; join with slip st to top of beginning ch-3, finish off.

SECOND MOTIF

Work same as First Motif through Rnd 4.

Rnd 5 (Joining rnd): Work beginning Shell, ch 5, holding **First Motif** with **right** side facing, slip st in center ch of any loop of **First Motif**, ch 5, 3 dc in next loop of **Second Motif**, ch 1, slip st in center ch of next Shell (ch-3 sp) on **First Motif**, ch 1, 3 dc in same loop on **Second Motif**, ch 5, slip st in center ch of next loop on **First Motif**, ch 5, (work Shell in next loop, ch 11) around; join with slip st to top of beginning ch-3, finish off.

Work **Third Motif** in same manner, skipping 2 Shells on **Second Motif** when joining.

BORDER

Rnd 1: With **right** side facing, join thread with slip st in first Shell on center Motif; work beginning Shell, † ch 2, dc in next loop, (ch 1, dc in same loop) 6 times, ch 2, work Shell in next Shell, ch 5, work Shell in next Shell, [ch 2, dc in next loop, (ch 1, dc in same loop) 6 times, ch 2, work Shell in next Shell] 4 times, ch 5 †, work Shell in next Shell, repeat from † to † once; join with slip st to top of beginning ch-3.

Rnd 2: Slip st in next 2 dc and in first ch-3 sp, work beginning Shell, † ch 3, sc in next dc, (sc in next ch-1 sp, sc in next dc) 6 times, ch 3, work Shell in next Shell, ch 3, sc in next loop, ch 3, work Shell in next Shell, ch 3, [sc in next dc, (sc in next ch-1 sp, sc in next dc) 6 times, ch 3, work Shell in next Shell, ch 3] 4 times, sc in next loop, ch 3 †, work Shell in next Shell, repeat from † to † once; join with slip st to top of beginning ch-3.

Rnd 3: Slip st in next 2 dc and in next 2 chs, work beginning Shell, † ch 3, sc in next sc, ch 3, (skip next sc, sc in next sc, ch 3) 6 times, work (Shell, ch 3, 3 dc) in each of next 2 Shells, ch 3, sc in next sc, ch 3, (skip next sc, sc in next sc, ch 3) 6 times, [work (Shell, ch 3, 3 dc) in next Shell, ch 3, sc in next sc, ch 3, (skip next sc, sc in next sc, ch 3) 6 times] 3 times †, work (Shell, ch 3, 3 dc) in each of next 2 Shells, repeat from † to † once, work (Shell, ch 3, 3 dc) in next Shell, 3 dc in same sp as beginning Shell, ch 3; join with slip st to top of beginning ch-3.

Rnd 4: Slip st in next 2 dc and in first ch-3 sp, work beginning Shell, † ch 3, skip next ch-3 sp, (sc in next ch-3 sp, ch 3) 6 times, skip next ch-3 sp, work Shell in next ch-3 sp, ch 3, work Cluster in each of next 2 ch-3 sps, ch 3, work Shell in next ch-3 sp, ch 3, skip next ch-3 sp, (sc in next ch-3 sp, ch 3) 6 times, skip next ch-3 sp, [work Shell in next 2 ch-3 sps, ch 3, skip next ch-3 sp, (sc in next ch-3 sp, ch 3) 6 times, skip next ch-3 sp] 3 times, work Shell in next ch-3 sp, ch 3, work Cluster in each of next 2 ch-3 sps, ch 3 †, work Shell in next ch-3 sp, repeat from † to † once; join with slip st to top of beginning ch-3.

Rnd 5: Slip st in next 2 dc and in first ch-3 sp, work beginning Shell, † ch 3, skip next ch-3 sp, (sc in next ch-3 sp, ch 3) 5 times, work Shell in next Shell, ch 7, work Shell in next Shell, ch 3, skip next ch-3 sp, (sc in next ch-3 sp, ch 3) 5 times, [(work Shell in next Shell, ch 3) twice, skip next ch-3 sp, (sc in next ch-3 sp, ch 3) 5 times] 3 times, work Shell in next Shell, ch 7 †, work Shell in next Shell, repeat from † to † once; join with slip st to top of beginning ch-3.

Rnd 6: Slip st in next 2 dc and in first ch-3 sp, work beginning Shell, † ch 4, skip next ch-3 sp, sc in next ch-3 sp, (ch 3, sc in next ch-3 sp) 3 times, ch 4, work Shell in next Shell, ch 5, (dc, ch 3, dc) in center ch of next loop, ch 5, work Shell in next Shell, ch 4, skip next ch-3 sp, sc in next ch-3 sp, (ch 3, sc in next ch-3 sp) 3 times, ch 4, work Shell in next Shell, ★ ch 2, (dc, ch 3, dc) in center ch of next loop, ch 2, work Shell in next Shell, ch 4, skip next ch-3 sp, sc in next ch-3 sp, (ch 3, sc in next ch-3 sp) 3 times, ch 4, work Shell in next Shell; repeat from ★ 2 times **more**, ch 5, (dc, ch 3, dc) in center ch of next loop, ch 5 †, work Shell in next Shell, repeat from † to † once; join with slip st to top of beginning ch-3.

Rnd 7: Slip st in next 2 dc and in first ch-3 sp, work beginning Shell, † ch 4, skip next loop, sc in next ch-3 sp, (ch 3, sc in next ch-3 sp) twice, ch 4, work Shell in next Shell, ch 5, skip next ch-5 sp, dc in next dc, 5 dc in next ch-3 sp, dc in next dc, ch 5, work Shell in next Shell, ch 4, skip next loop, sc in next ch-3 sp, (ch 3, sc in next ch-3 sp) twice, ch 4, work Shell in next Shell, ★ ch 3, skip next ch-2 sp, dc in next dc, 5 dc in next ch-3 sp, dc in next dc, ch 3, work Shell in next Shell, ch 4, skip next loop, sc in next ch-3 sp, (ch 3, sc in next ch-3 sp) twice, ch 4, work Shell in next Shell; repeat from ★ 2 times **more**, ch 5, skip next loop, dc in next dc, 5 dc in next ch-3 sp, dc in next dc, ch 5 †, work Shell in next Shell, repeat from † to † once; join with slip st to top of beginning ch-3.

Rnd 8: Slip st in next 2 dc and in first ch-3 sp, work beginning Shell, † ch 5, skip next loop, sc in next ch-3 sp, ch 3, sc in next ch-3 sp, ch 5, work Shell in next Shell, ch 6, skip next loop, sc in next dc, work Picot, sc in next 5 dc, work Picot, sc in next dc, ch 6, work Shell in next Shell, ch 5, skip next loop, sc in next ch-3 sp, ch 3, sc in next ch-3 sp, ch 5, work Shell in next Shell, ★ ch 4, skip next loop, sc in next dc, work Picot, sc in next 5 dc, work Picot, sc in next dc, ch 4, work Shell in next Shell, ch 5, skip next loop, sc in next ch-3 sp, ch 3, sc in next ch-3 sp, ch 5, work Shell in next Shell; repeat from ★ 2 times **more**, ch 6, skip next loop, sc in next dc, work Picot, sc in next 5 dc, work Picot, sc in next dc, ch 6 †, work Shell in next Shell, repeat from † to † once; join with slip st to top of beginning ch-3.

Rnd 9: Slip st in next 2 dc and in next 2 chs, work beginning Shell, † ch 5, skip next loop, sc in next ch-3 sp, ch 5, work (Shell, ch 3, 3 dc) in next Shell, ch 7, skip next Picot and next sc, dc in next 3 sc, ch 7, work (Shell, ch 3, 3 dc) in next Shell, ch 5, skip next loop, sc in next ch-3 sp, ch 5, work (Shell, ch 3, 3 dc) in next Shell, ★ ch 6, skip next Picot and next sc, dc in next 3 sc, ch 6, work (Shell, ch 3, 3 dc) in next Shell, ch 5, skip next loop, sc in next ch-3 sp, ch 5, work (Shell, ch 3, 3 dc) in next Shell; repeat from ★ 2 times **more**, ch 7, skip next Picot and next sc, dc in next 3 dc, ch 7 †, work (Shell, ch 3, 3 dc) in next Shell, repeat from † to † once, 3 dc in same sp as beginning Shell, ch 3; join with slip st to top of beginning ch-3.

Rnd 10: Slip st in next 2 dc and in first ch-3 sp, work beginning Shell, work Shell in next ch-3 sp, † ch 3, work Shell in next ch-3 sp, ch 6, skip next loop, sc in next 3 dc, ch 6, work Shell in next ch-3 sp, ch 3, work Shell in next 2 ch-3 sps, ch 3, work Shell in next ch-3 sp, ★ ch 5, skip next loop, sc in next 3 dc, ch 5, work Shell in next ch-3 sp, ch 3, work Shell in next 2 ch-3 sps, ch 3, work Shell in next ch-3 sp; repeat from ★ 2 times **more**, ch 6, skip next loop, sc in next 3 dc, ch 6, work Shell in next ch-3 sp †, ch 3, work Shell in next 2 ch-3 sps, repeat from † to † once, ch 1, hdc in top of beginning ch-3 to form last sp.

Rnd 11: Ch 1, sc in same sp, † ch 6, work Cluster in each of next 2 Shells, ch 6, sc in next ch-3 sp, ch 6, work Shell in next Shell, ch 5, sc in next sc, ch 4, skip next sc, sc in next sc, ch 5, work Shell in next Shell, ch 6, sc in next ch-3 sp, ch 6, work Cluster in each of next 2 Shells, ch 6, sc in next ch-3 sp, ch 6, work Shell in next Shell, ★ ch 3, sc in next sc, ch 4, skip next sc, sc in next sc, ch 3, work Shell in next Shell, ch 6, sc in next ch-3 sp, ch 6, work Cluster in each of next 2 Shells, ch 6, sc in next ch-3 sp, ch 6, work Shell in next Shell; repeat from ★ 2 times **more**, ch 5, sc in next sc, ch 4, skip next sc, sc in next sc, ch 5, work Shell in next Shell †, ch 6, sc in next ch-3 sp, repeat from † to † once, ch 3, dc in first sc to form last loop.

Rnd 12: Ch 1, sc in same loop, ch 7, (sc in next loop, ch 7) 3 times, work Shell in next Shell, ch 3, skip next loop, sc in next loop, ch 3, work Shell in next Shell, ★ ch 7, (sc in next loop, ch 7) 4 times, work Shell in next Shell, ch 3, skip next loop, sc in next loop, ch 3, work Shell in next Shell; repeat from ★ around, ch 3, tr in first sc to form last loop.

Rnd 13: Ch 1, sc in same loop, ch 7, (sc in next loop, ch 7) 4 times, work Shell in next 2 Shells, ★ ch 7, (sc in next loop, ch 7) 5 times, work Shell in next 2 Shells; repeat from ★ around, ch 3, tr in first sc to form last loop.

Rnd 14: Ch 1, sc in same loop, ch 7, (sc in next loop, ch 7) 5 times, work Cluster in each of next 2 Shells, ★ ch 7, (sc in next loop, ch 7) 6 times, work Cluster in each of next 2 Shells; repeat from ★ around, ch 3, tr in first sc to form last loop.

Rnd 15: Ch 1, sc in same loop, (ch 7, sc in next loop) 3 times, ch 3, sc in **same** loop, ★ (ch 7, sc in next loop) 7 times, ch 3, sc in **same** loop; repeat from ★ around to last 3 loops, (ch 7, sc in next loop) 3 times, ch 3, tr in first sc to form last loop.

Rnd 16: Ch 1, sc in same loop, (ch 7, sc in next loop) 3 times, ch 1, work Shell in next ch-3 sp, ch 1, sc in next loop, ★ (ch 7, sc in next loop) 6 times, ch 1, work Shell in next ch-3 sp, ch 1, sc in next loop; repeat from ★ around to last 2 loops, (ch 7, sc in next loop) twice, ch 3, tr in first sc to form last loop.

Rnd 17: Ch 1, sc in same loop, ch 8, (sc in next loop, ch 8) 3 times, skip next 2 dc, sc in next dc, ch 5, sc in next dc, ★ ch 8, (sc in next loop, ch 8) 6 times, skip next 2 dc, sc in next dc, ch 5, sc in next dc; repeat from ★ around to last 2 loops, (ch 8, sc in next loop) twice, ch 4, tr in first sc to form last loop.

Rnds 18 and 19: Ch 1, sc in same loop, (ch 8, sc in next loop) around, ch 4, tr in first sc to form last loop.

Rnd 20: Ch 1, sc in same loop, ch 8, (sc in next loop, ch 8) around; join with slip st to first sc.

Rnd 21: Ch 4, (tr, ch 4, 2 tr) in same st, sc in next loop, ch 8, sc in next loop, ★ (2 tr, ch 4, 2 tr) in next sc, sc in next loop, ch 8, sc in next loop; repeat from ★ around; join with slip st to top of beginning ch-4.

Rnd 22: Slip st in next tr and in first ch-4 sp, ch 4, (2 tr, ch 6, slip st in fifth ch from hook, ch 1, 3 tr) in same sp, ch 4, (sc, work Picot, sc) in next loop, ch 4, ★ (3 tr, ch 6, slip st in fifth ch from hook, ch 1, 3 tr) in next ch-4 sp, ch 4, (sc, work Picot, sc) in next loop, ch 4; repeat from ★ around; join with slip st to top of beginning ch-4, finish off.

4

Finished Size: Approximately 12½″ in diameter

MATERIALS
Bedspread Weight Cotton Thread (size 10),
  approximately 155 yards
Steel crochet hook, size 6 (1.50 mm) **or** size needed
  for gauge

GAUGE: Rnds 1-4 = 2″

PATTERN STITCHES
Picot: Ch 3, slip st in stitch just made.

Treble Crochet (abbreviated tr): YO twice, insert hook
in stitch or space indicated, YO and pull up a loop
(4 loops on hook), (YO and draw through 2 loops on
hook) 3 times.

Ch 8, join with slip st to form a ring.

Rnd 1 (Right side)**:** Ch 3, 15 dc in ring; join with slip st
to top of beginning ch-3: 16 sts.

Rnd 2: Ch 3, dc in same st, ch 2, skip next dc, (2 dc in
next dc, ch 2, skip next dc) around; join with slip st to
top of beginning ch-3: 8 ch-2 sps.

Rnd 3: Ch 3, dc in same st, 2 dc in next dc, ch 2,
(2 dc in each of next 2 dc, ch 2) around; join with slip st
to top of beginning ch-3.

Rnd 4: Ch 3, dc in same st, dc in next 2 dc, 2 dc in
next dc, ch 2, (2 dc in next dc, dc in next 2 dc, 2 dc in
next dc, ch 2) around; join with slip st to top of
beginning ch-3.

Rnd 5: Ch 3, dc in next 2 dc, ch 3, dc in next 3 dc,
ch 2, (dc in next 3 dc, ch 3, dc in next 3 dc, ch 2)
around; join with slip st to top of beginning ch-3.

Rnd 6: Ch 3, dc in next 2 dc, ch 3, dc in next ch-3 sp, ch 3, dc in next 3 dc, ch 2, ★ dc in next 3 dc, ch 3, dc in next ch-3 sp, ch 3, dc in next 3 dc, ch 2; repeat from ★ around; join with slip st to top of beginning ch-3.

Rnd 7: Ch 3, dc in next 2 dc, ch 3, (dc, ch 3, dc) in next dc, ch 3, dc in next 3 dc, ch 2, ★ dc in next 3 dc, ch 3, (dc, ch 3, dc) in next dc, ch 3, dc in next 3 dc, ch 2; repeat from ★ around; join with slip st to top of beginning ch-3.

Rnd 8: Ch 3, dc in next 2 dc, ch 5, skip next ch-3 sp, dc in center ch of next ch-3 sp, (ch 1, dc) twice in **same** st, ch 5, skip next ch-3 sp, dc in next 3 dc, ch 2, ★ dc in next 3 dc, ch 5, skip next ch-3 sp, dc in center ch of next ch-3 sp, (ch 1, dc) twice in **same** st, ch 5, skip next ch-3 sp, dc in next 3 dc, ch 2; repeat from ★ around; join with slip st to top of beginning ch-3.

Rnd 9: Ch 3, dc in next 2 dc, ch 3, 2 dc in next dc, (ch 2, 2 dc in next dc) twice, ch 3, dc in next 3 dc, ch 2, ★ dc in next 3 dc, ch 3, 2 dc in next dc, (ch 2, 2 dc in next dc) twice, ch 3, dc in next 3 dc, ch 2; repeat from ★ around; join with slip st to top of beginning ch-3.

Rnd 10: Ch 3, dc in next 2 dc, ★ † ch 3, dc in next dc, work Picot, dc in next dc, ch 3, 2 dc in each of next 2 dc, ch 3, dc in next dc, work Picot, dc in next dc, ch 3, dc in next 3 dc, ch 2 †, dc in next 3 dc; repeat from ★ 6 times **more**, then repeat from † to † once; join with slip st to top of beginning ch-3.

Rnd 11: Ch 4, tr in next 2 dc, ★ † ch 6, skip next 2 dc, dc in next dc, (ch 1, dc in next dc) 3 times, ch 6, skip next 2 dc, tr in next 3 dc, ch 2 †, tr in next 3 dc; repeat from ★ 6 times **more**, then repeat from † to † once; join with slip st to top of beginning ch-4.

Note: Work 3-tr Cluster as follows: ★ YO twice, insert hook in dc indicated, YO and pull up a loop, (YO and draw through 2 loops on hook) twice; repeat from ★ 2 times **more**, YO and draw through all 4 loops on hook.

Rnd 12: Ch 4, tr in next 2 tr, ★ † ch 4, work 3-tr Cluster in next dc, (ch 3, work 3-tr Cluster in next dc) 3 times, ch 4, tr in next 3 tr, ch 2 †, tr in next 3 tr; repeat from ★ 6 times **more**, then repeat from † to † once; join with slip st to top of beginning ch-4.

Rnd 13: Ch 4, tr in next 2 tr, ★ † ch 4, sc in next loop, (ch 5, sc in next loop) 4 times, ch 4, tr in next 3 tr, ch 3, tr in next ch-2 sp, ch 3 †, tr in next 3 tr; repeat from ★ 6 times **more**, then repeat from † to † once; join with slip st to top of beginning ch-4.

Rnd 14: Ch 4, tr in next tr, ★ † 2 tr in next tr, ch 4, skip next loop, sc in next loop, (ch 5, sc in next loop) 3 times, ch 4, 2 tr in next tr, tr in next 2 tr, ch 3, (tr in next ch-3 sp, ch 3) twice †, tr in next 2 tr; repeat from ★ 6 times **more**, then repeat from † to † once; join with slip st to top of beginning ch-4.

Rnd 15: Ch 4, tr in next 3 tr, ★ † ch 4, skip next loop, sc in next loop, (ch 5, sc in next loop) twice, ch 4, tr in next 4 tr, ch 3, (tr in next ch-3 sp, ch 3) 3 times †, tr in next 4 tr; repeat from ★ 6 times **more**, then repeat from † to † once; join with slip st to top of beginning ch-4.

Rnd 16: Ch 4, tr in next 3 tr, ★ † ch 4, skip next loop, sc in next loop, ch 5, sc in next loop, ch 4, tr in next 4 tr, ch 3, (tr in next ch-3 sp, work Picot, ch 3) 4 times †, tr in next 4 tr; repeat from ★ 6 times **more**, then repeat from † to † once; join with slip st to top of beginning ch-4.

Rnd 17: Ch 4, tr in next 3 tr, ★ † ch 4, skip next loop, sc in next loop, ch 4, tr in next 4 tr, ch 3, (tr in next ch-3 sp, work Picot, ch 3) 5 times †, tr in next 4 tr; repeat from ★ 6 times **more**, then repeat from † to † once; join with slip st to top of beginning ch-4.

Rnd 18: Ch 4, tr in next 7 tr, ch 4, (tr in next ch-3 sp, work Picot, ch 4) 6 times, ★ tr in next 8 tr, ch 4, (tr in next ch-3 sp, work Picot, ch 4) 6 times; repeat from ★ around; join with slip st to top of beginning ch-4.

Note: Decrease as follows: ★ YO, insert hook in **next** tr, YO and pull up a loop, YO and draw through 2 loops on hook; repeat from ★ once **more**, YO and draw through all 3 loops on hook.

Rnd 19: Ch 2, dc in next 2 tr, decrease, dc in next tr, decrease, ch 4, (tr in next ch-4 sp, work Picot, ch 4) 7 times, ★ decrease, (dc in next tr, decrease) twice, ch 4, (tr in next ch-4 sp, work Picot, ch 4) 7 times; repeat from ★ around; join with slip st to first dc.

Note #1: Work beginning Cluster as follows: Ch 2, ★ YO, insert hook in **next** stitch, YO and pull up a loop, YO and draw through 2 loops on hook; repeat from ★ 3 times **more**, YO and draw through all 5 loops on hook.

Note #2: Work Cluster as follows: ★ YO, insert hook in **next** stitch, YO and pull up a loop, YO and draw through 2 loops on hook; repeat from ★ 4 times **more**, YO and draw through all 6 loops on hook.

Rnd 20: Work beginning Cluster, ch 5, (tr in next ch-4 sp, work Picot, ch 5) 8 times, ★ work Cluster, ch 5, (tr in next ch-4 sp, work Picot, ch 5) 8 times; repeat from ★ around; join with slip st to beginning Cluster, finish off.

6

PATTERN STITCHES

Treble Crochet *(abbreviated tr)*: YO twice, insert hook in stitch indicated, YO and pull up a loop (4 loops on hook), (YO and draw through 2 loops on hook) 3 times.

Beginning Cluster: Ch 3, ★ YO twice, insert hook in stitch or space indicated and pull up a loop, (YO and draw through 2 loops on hook) twice; repeat from ★ once **more**, YO and draw through all 3 loops on hook.

Cluster: ★ YO twice, insert hook in stitch or space indicated and pull up a loop, (YO and draw through 2 loops on hook) twice; repeat from ★ 2 times **more**, YO and draw through all 4 loops on hook.

Picot: Ch 3, slip st in stitch just made.

Double Treble Crochet *(abbreviated dtr)*: YO 3 times, insert hook in space indicated, YO and pull up a loop (5 loops on hook), (YO and draw through 2 loops on hook) 4 times.

Shell: Work (Cluster, ch 3, Cluster) in stitch or space indicated.

Finished Size: Approximately 14" x 14"

MATERIALS

Bedspread Weight Cotton Thread (size 10), approximately:
    MC (Ecru) - 130 yards
    CC (Green) - 130 yards
Steel crochet hook, size 6 (1.50 mm) **or** size needed for gauge

GAUGE: Rnds 1-6 = 3¼"

With MC ch 10, join with slip st to form a ring.

Rnd 1 (Right side)**:** Ch 1, 20 sc in ring; join with slip st to first sc.

Note: Loop a short piece of thread around any stitch to mark last round as **right** side.

Rnd 2: Ch 7, tr in next sc, (ch 3, tr in next sc) around, ch 1, hdc in fourth ch of beginning ch-7 to form last sp: 20 ch-3 sps.

7

Rnd 3: Ch 1, sc in same sp, (ch 3, sc in next ch-3 sp) around, ch 1, hdc in first sc to form last sp.

Rnd 4: Ch 1, sc in same sp, (ch 4, sc in next ch-3 sp) around, ch 2, hdc in first sc to form last loop: 20 loops.

Rnd 5: Ch 1, sc in same loop, (ch 4, sc in next loop) around, ch 2, hdc in first sc to form last loop.

Rnd 6: Work beginning Cluster in same loop, (ch 5, work Cluster in next loop) around, ch 2, dc in beginning Cluster to form last loop.

Rnd 7: Ch 1, sc in same loop, (ch 6, sc in next loop) around, ch 3, dc in first sc to form last loop.

Rnd 8: Ch 1, (sc, work Picot, sc) in same loop, ★ ch 6, (sc, work Picot, sc) in next loop; repeat from ★ around, ch 3, dc in first sc to form last loop.

Rnd 9: Ch 1, sc in same loop, (ch 9, sc in next loop) around, ch 5, tr in first sc to form last loop.

Rnd 10: Ch 1, (sc, work Picot, sc) in same loop, tr in next sc, ch 7, dc in fifth ch from hook (loop made), ch 3, tr in same sc, ★ (sc, work Picot, sc) in next loop, tr in next sc, ch 7, dc in fifth ch from hook, ch 3, tr in same sc; repeat from ★ around; join with slip st to first sc, finish off.

Rnd 11: With **right** side facing, join CC with slip st in any loop; work (beginning Cluster, ch 5, Cluster) in same loop, ch 5, (work Cluster, ch 5) twice in each loop around; join with slip st to beginning Cluster.

Rnd 12: Slip st in first loop, work beginning Cluster, ch 3, (work Cluster, ch 3) 3 times in same loop, sc in next loop, ch 3, ★ (work Cluster, ch 3) 4 times in next loop, sc in next loop, ch 3; repeat from ★ around; join with slip st to beginning Cluster.

Rnd 13: Ch 1, sc in same st, (2 sc, work Picot, sc) in next ch-3 sp, sc in next Cluster, ★ † ch 20, sc in next Cluster, (2 sc, work Picot, sc) in next ch-3 sp, sc in next Cluster, ch 5, sc in next Cluster, (2 sc, work Picot, sc) in next ch-3 sp, sc in next Cluster, ch 8, sc in next Cluster, (2 sc, work Picot, sc) in next ch-3 sp, sc in next Cluster, [ch 5, sc in next Cluster, (2 sc, work Picot, sc) in next ch-3 sp, sc in next Cluster] 5 times, ch 8, sc in next Cluster, (2 sc, work Picot, sc) in next ch-3 sp, sc in next Cluster, ch 5 †, sc in next Cluster, (2 sc, work Picot, sc) in next ch-3 sp, sc in next Cluster; repeat from ★ 2 times **more**, then repeat from † to † once; join with slip st to first sc, finish off.

Rnd 14: With **right** side facing, join MC with slip st in any ch-20 loop; ch 7, dtr in same loop, ★ † ch 13, skip next loop, dc in next loop, ch 13, (skip next loop, sc in next loop, ch 13) twice, skip next loop, dc in next loop, ch 13, skip next loop †, (dtr, ch 2, dtr, ch 5, dtr, ch 2, dtr) in next loop; repeat from ★ 2 times **more**, then repeat from † to † once, (dtr, ch 2, dtr) in first loop, ch 2, dc in fifth ch of beginning ch-7 to form last loop.

Rnd 15: Ch 6, skip next st, ★ † work Shell in next dtr, (ch 3, tr in center ch of next loop, ch 3, work Shell in next st) 5 times, ch 2, skip next dtr †, (tr, ch 5, tr) in center ch of next loop, ch 2, skip next dtr; repeat from ★ 2 times **more**, then repeat from † to † once, tr in same st as beginning ch-6, ch 2, dc in fourth ch of beginning ch-6 to form last loop.

Rnd 16: Ch 5, dc in next st, ★ † ch 1, dc in next ch-2 sp, ch 1, dc in next st, ch 1, (dc in center ch of next ch-3 sp, ch 1, dc in next st, ch 1) 16 times, dc in next ch-2 sp, ch 1, dc in next tr, ch 2 †, (dc, ch 5, dc) in center ch of next loop, ch 2, dc in next tr; repeat from ★ 2 times **more**, then repeat from † to † once, dc in same st as beginning ch-5, ch 2, dc in third ch of beginning ch-5 to form last loop.

Rnd 17: Ch 7, skip next st, ★ † work Shell in next dc, ch 3, [skip next 2 dc, tr in next dc, ch 3, skip next 2 dc, work Shell in next dc, ch 3] 6 times, skip next dc †, (tr, ch 5, tr) in center ch of next loop, ch 3, skip next dc; repeat from ★ 2 times **more**, then repeat from † to † once, tr in same st as beginning ch-7, ch 2, dc in fourth ch of beginning ch-7 to form last loop.

Rnd 18: Ch 5, dc in next st, ★ † (ch 1, dc in center ch of next ch-3 sp, ch 1, dc in next st) 21 times, ch 2 †, (dc, ch 5, dc) in center ch of next loop, ch 2, dc in next tr; repeat from ★ 2 times **more**, then repeat from † to † once, dc in same st as beginning ch-5, ch 2, dc in third ch of beginning ch-5 to form last loop.

Rnd 19: Ch 7, skip next st, ★ † work Shell in next dc, ch 3, [skip next 2 dc, tr in next dc, ch 3, skip next 2 dc, work Shell in next dc, ch 3] 7 times, skip next dc †, (tr, ch 5, tr) in center ch of next loop, ch 3, skip next dc; repeat from ★ 2 times **more**, then repeat from † to † once, tr in same st as beginning ch-7, ch 2, dc in fourth ch of beginning ch-7 to form last loop.

Rnd 20: Ch 8, dc in same st, ★ † ch 2, dc in next st, (ch 1, dc in center ch of next ch-3 sp, ch 1, dc in next st) 24 times, ch 2 †, (dc, ch 5, dc) in center ch of next loop; repeat from ★ 2 times **more**, then repeat from † to † once; join with slip st to third ch of beginning ch-8, finish off.

Rnd 21: With **right** side facing, join CC with slip st in center ch of any corner loop; ch 6, ★ † skip next dc, work Shell in next dc, (ch 7, skip next 5 dc, work Shell in next dc) 8 times, ch 2, skip next dc †, (tr, ch 5, tr) in center ch of next loop, ch 2; repeat from ★ 2 times **more**, then repeat from † to † once, tr in same st as beginning ch-6, ch 2, dc in fourth ch of beginning ch-6 to form last loop.

Rnd 22: Ch 1, sc in same st, ch 3, ★ † work (Shell, ch 3, Shell) in next Shell (ch-3 sp), ch 3, [sc in center ch of next loop, ch 3, work (Shell, ch 3, Shell) in next Shell, ch 3] 8 times †, skip next ch-2 sp, sc in center ch of next loop, ch 3; repeat from ★ 2 times **more**, then repeat from † to † once; join with slip st to first sc.

Rnd 23: Ch 1, sc in same st, ★ † work Picot, 3 sc in next ch-3 sp, sc in next Cluster, (2 sc, work Picot, sc) in next ch-3 sp, sc in next Cluster, (2 sc, ch 5, slip st in sc just made, sc) in next ch-3 sp, sc in next Cluster, (2 sc, work Picot, sc) in next ch-3 sp, sc in next Cluster, 3 sc in next ch-3 sp †, sc in next sc; repeat from ★ around to last 5 ch-3 sps, then repeat from † to † once; join with slip st to first sc, finish off.

8

April   *Tiffany*

PATTERN STITCHES

2-dc Cluster: YO, insert hook in **same** space, YO and pull up a loop, YO and draw through 2 loops on hook, YO, insert hook in **next** space, YO and pull up a loop, YO and draw through 2 loops on hook, YO and draw through all 3 loops on hook.

Beginning Cluster: Ch 3, ★ YO, insert hook in **same** stitch and pull up a loop, YO and draw through 2 loops on hook; repeat from ★ once **more**, YO and draw through all 3 loops on hook.

Cluster: ★ YO, insert hook in stitch or space indicated and pull up a loop, YO and draw through 2 loops on hook; repeat from ★ 2 times **more**, YO and draw through all 4 loops on hook.

Treble Crochet *(abbreviated tr)*: YO twice, insert hook in stitch or space indicated, YO and pull up a loop (4 loops on hook), (YO and draw through 2 loops on hook) 3 times.

Shell: (2 dc, ch 3, 2 dc) in stitch or space indicated.

Finished Size: Approximately 17″ in diameter

MATERIALS
Bedspread Weight Cotton Thread (size 10), approximately 1 ball (282 yards per ball)
Steel crochet hook, size 6 (1.50 mm) **or** size needed for gauge

GAUGE: Rnds 1-4 = 2″

Ch 8, join with slip st to form a ring.

Rnd 1 (Right side): Ch 3, 17 dc in ring; join with slip st to beginning ch-3: 18 sts.

Rnd 2: Ch 5, (dc in next dc, ch 2) around; join with slip st to third ch of beginning ch-5.

Rnd 3: Slip st in first sp, ch 1, sc in same sp, (ch 3, sc in next sp) around, ch 1, hdc in first sc to form last sp: 18 sps.

Rnd 4: Ch 2, dc in next ch-3 sp, (ch 3, work 2-dc Cluster) around, ch 1, hdc in first dc to form last sp.

Rnd 5: Ch 2, dc in next ch-3 sp, (ch 4, work 2-dc Cluster) around, ch 2, hdc in first dc to form last sp.

Rnd 6: Ch 2, dc in next ch-4 sp, ch 5, (work 2-dc Cluster, ch 5) around; join with slip st to first dc.

Rnd 7: Work (beginning Cluster, ch 3, Cluster) in same st, ch 3, ★ work (Cluster, ch 3, Cluster) in next 2-dc Cluster, ch 3; repeat from ★ around; join with slip st to beginning Cluster: 36 Clusters.

Rnd 8: Slip st in first ch-3 sp, ch 11, skip next ch-3 sp, (tr in next ch-3 sp, ch 7, skip next ch-3 sp) around; join with slip st to fourth ch of beginning ch-11: 18 loops.

Rnd 9: Ch 3, 9 dc in first loop, (dc in next tr, 9 dc in next loop) around; join with slip st to top of beginning ch-3: 180 sts.

Rnd 10: Ch 3, dc in next dc, ★ † ch 5, skip next 5 dc, work Cluster in next dc, (ch 2, skip next 2 dc, work Cluster in next dc) twice, ch 5, skip next 5 dc †, dc in next 3 dc; repeat from ★ 7 times **more**, then repeat from † to † once, dc in last dc; join with slip st to top of beginning ch-3.

Rnd 11: Ch 3, dc in next dc, ★ † ch 5, work Cluster in next sp, (ch 2, work Cluster in next sp) 3 times, ch 5 †, dc in next 3 dc; repeat from ★ 7 times **more**, then repeat from † to † once, dc in last dc; join with slip st to top of beginning ch-3.

Rnd 12: Ch 3, dc in next dc, ★ † ch 5, work Cluster in next sp, (ch 2, work Cluster in next sp) 4 times, ch 5 †, dc in next 3 dc; repeat from ★ 7 times **more**, then repeat from † to † once, dc in last dc; join with slip st to top of beginning ch-3.

Rnd 13: Ch 3, dc in next dc, ★ † ch 5, work Cluster in next sp, (ch 2, work Cluster in next sp) 5 times, ch 5, dc in next dc †, 2 dc in next dc, dc in next dc; repeat from ★ 7 times **more**, then repeat from † to † once, dc in same dc as beginning ch-3; join with slip st to top of beginning ch-3.

Rnd 14: Ch 4, tr in same st, ★ † tr in next dc, ch 5, skip next sp, work Cluster in next sp, (ch 2, work Cluster in next sp) 4 times, ch 5, tr in next dc, 2 tr in next dc, ch 3 †, 2 tr in next dc; repeat from ★ 7 times **more**, then repeat from † to † once; join with slip st to top of beginning ch-4.

Rnd 15: Ch 4, tr in next 2 tr, ★ † ch 5, skip next sp, work Cluster in next sp, (ch 2, work Cluster in next sp) 3 times, ch 5, tr in next 3 tr, ch 7 †, tr in next 3 tr; repeat from ★ 7 times **more**, then repeat from † to † once; join with slip st to top of beginning ch-4.

Rnd 16: Ch 4, tr in next 2 tr, ★ † ch 5, skip next sp, work Cluster in next sp, (ch 2, work Cluster in next sp) twice, ch 5, tr in next 3 tr, ch 5, tr in next loop, ch 5 †, tr in next 3 tr; repeat from ★ 7 times **more**, then repeat from † to † once; join with slip st to top of beginning ch-4.

Rnd 17: Ch 4, tr in next 2 tr, ★ † ch 5, skip next sp, work Cluster in next sp, ch 2, work Cluster in next sp, ch 5, tr in next 3 tr, ch 5, work Shell in next tr, ch 5 †, tr in next 3 tr; repeat from ★ 7 times **more**, then repeat from † to † once; join with slip st to top of beginning ch-4.

Rnd 18: Ch 4, tr in next 2 tr, ★ † ch 5, skip next sp, work Cluster in next sp, ch 5, tr in next 3 tr, ch 5, (work Shell, ch 3, 2 dc) in next Shell (ch-3 sp), ch 5 †, tr in next 3 tr; repeat from ★ 7 times **more**, then repeat from † to † once; join with slip st to top of beginning ch-4.

Rnd 19: Ch 4, tr in next 2 tr, ★ † ch 5, sc in next Cluster, ch 5, tr in next 3 tr, ch 5, (work Shell in next ch-3 sp, ch 5) twice †, tr in next 3 tr; repeat from ★ 7 times **more**, then repeat from † to † once; join with slip st to top of beginning ch-4.

Rnd 20: Ch 4, tr in next 2 tr, ★ † ch 3, tr in next 3 tr, ch 5, work Shell in next Shell, ch 3, work Shell in center ch of next loop, ch 3, work Shell in next Shell, ch 5 †, tr in next 3 tr; repeat from ★ 7 times **more**, then repeat from † to † once; join with slip st to top of beginning ch-4.

Rnd 21: Ch 4, tr in next 5 tr, ★ † ch 5, work Shell in next Shell, ch 5, skip next ch-3 sp, dc in next 2 dc, 5 dc in next ch-3 sp, dc in next 2 dc, ch 5, work Shell in next Shell, ch 5 †, tr in next 6 tr; repeat from ★ 7 times **more**, then repeat from † to † once; join with slip st to top of beginning ch-4.

Note #1: Work beginning 6-tr Cluster as follows: Ch 3, ★ YO twice, insert hook in **next** tr, YO and pull up a loop, (YO and draw through 2 loops on hook) twice; repeat from ★ 4 times **more**, YO and draw through all 6 loops on hook.

Note #2: Work 6-tr Cluster as follows: ★ YO twice, insert hook in **next** tr, YO and pull up a loop, (YO and draw through 2 loops on hook) twice; repeat from ★ 5 times **more**, YO and draw through all 7 loops on hook.

Rnd 22: Work beginning 6-tr Cluster, ★ † ch 5, work Shell in next Shell, ch 7, skip next loop, (tr in next dc, ch 1) 3 times, (tr, ch 1) twice in next dc, tr in next dc, (ch 1, tr) twice in next dc, (ch 1, tr in next dc) 3 times, ch 7, work Shell in next Shell, ch 5 †, work 6-tr Cluster; repeat from ★ 7 times **more**, then repeat from † to † once; join with slip st to beginning 6-tr Cluster.

Rnd 23: Ch 1, sc in same st, ★ † ch 5, work Shell in next Shell, ch 4, (sc, ch 3, sc) in center ch of next loop, ch 4, dc in next tr, (ch 1, dc in next tr) 10 times, ch 4, (sc, ch 3, sc) in center ch of next loop, ch 4, work Shell in next Shell, ch 5 †, sc in next Cluster; repeat from ★ 7 times **more**, then repeat from † to † once; join with slip st to first sc.

Rnd 24: Slip st in next 5 chs and in next 2 dc, slip st in next ch-3 sp, ch 3, (dc, ch 3, 2 dc) in same sp, ★ † ch 7, skip next 2 sc, 4 dc in next dc, (ch 4, slip st in third ch from hook, ch 1, skip next dc, 4 dc in next dc) 5 times, ch 7, work Shell in next Shell, ch 5 †, work Shell in next Shell; repeat from ★ 7 times **more**, then repeat from † to † once; join with slip st to top of beginning ch-3.

Note: Work 4-tr Cluster as follows: ★ YO twice, insert hook in **next** dc, YO and pull up a loop, (YO and draw through 2 loops on hook) twice; repeat from ★ 3 times **more**, YO and draw through all 5 loops on hook.

Rnd 25: Slip st in next dc and in next ch-3 sp, ch 3, (dc, ch 3, 2 dc) in same sp, ★ † ch 4, (sc, ch 3, sc) in center ch of next loop, ch 4, work 4-tr Cluster, (ch 7, slip st in fourth ch from hook, ch 3, work 4-tr Cluster) 5 times, ch 4, (sc, ch 3, sc) in center ch of next loop, ch 4 †, work Shell in each of next 2 Shells; repeat from ★ 7 times **more**, then repeat from † to † once, work Shell in next Shell; join with slip st to top of beginning ch-3, finish off.

May

Photographed on Front Cover.

Finished Size: Approximately 14½" x 20"

MATERIALS
Bedspread Weight Cotton Thread (size 10),
  approximately 1 ball (282 yards per ball)
Steel crochet hook, size 6 (1.50 mm) **or** size needed
  for gauge

GAUGE: Rnds 1-4 = 2¼"

PATTERN STITCHES
2-dc Cluster: YO, insert hook in **same** dc, YO and pull
up a loop, YO and draw through 2 loops on hook, YO,
insert hook in **next** dc, YO and pull up a loop, YO and
draw through 2 loops on hook, YO and draw through all
3 loops on hook.

3-dc Cluster: ★ YO, insert hook in space indicated and
pull up a loop, YO and draw through 2 loops on hook;
repeat from ★ 2 times **more**, YO and draw through all
4 loops on hook.

Treble Crochet *(abbreviated tr)*: YO twice, insert hook
in stitch or space indicated, YO and pull up a loop
(4 loops on hook), (YO and draw through 2 loops on
hook) 3 times.

V-St: (Tr, ch 3, tr) in stitch indicated.

Picot: Ch 3, slip st in stitch just made.

4-tr Cluster: ★ YO twice, insert hook in **next** tr, YO
and pull up a loop, (YO and draw through 2 loops on
hook) twice; repeat from ★ 3 times **more**, YO and draw
through all 5 loops on hook.

BODY
Ch 8, join with slip st to form a ring.

Rnd 1 (Right side)**:** Ch 3, 3 dc in ring, ch 3, (4 dc in
ring, ch 3) 3 times; join with slip st to top of beginning
ch-3: 4 ch-3 sps.

Note: Loop a short piece of thread around any stitch to
mark last round as **right** side.

Rnd 2: Ch 3, dc in next 3 dc, ch 2, (dc, ch 3, dc) in
center ch of next ch-3, ch 2, ★ dc in next 4 dc, ch 2,
(dc, ch 3, dc) in center ch of next ch-3, ch 2; repeat
from ★ 2 times **more**; join with slip st to top of
beginning ch-3.

Rnd 3: Ch 3, dc in next 3 dc, ch 2, skip next ch-2 sp,
7 dc in next ch-3 sp, ch 2, ★ dc in next 4 dc, ch 2, skip
next ch-2 sp, 7 dc in next ch-3 sp, ch 2; repeat from ★
2 times **more**; join with slip st to top of beginning ch-3.

Rnd 4: Ch 3, dc in next 3 dc, ch 3, 2 dc in next dc, dc
in next 5 dc, 2 dc in next dc, ch 3, ★ dc in next 4 dc,
ch 3, 2 dc in next dc, dc in next 5 dc, 2 dc in next dc,
ch 3; repeat from ★ 2 times **more**; join with slip st to
beginning ch-3.

Rnd 5: Ch 3, dc in next 3 dc, ch 3, dc in next dc,
(ch 1, dc in next dc) 8 times, ch 3, ★ dc in next 4 dc,
ch 3, dc in next dc, (ch 1, dc in next dc) 8 times, ch 3;
repeat from ★ 2 times **more**; join with slip st to top of
beginning ch-3.

Rnd 6: Ch 3, dc in next 3 dc, ch 3, dc in next dc,
ch 2, (work 2-dc Cluster, ch 2) 8 times, dc in **same** dc,
ch 3, ★ dc in next 4 dc, ch 3, dc in next dc, ch 2,
(work 2-dc Cluster, ch 2) 8 times, dc in **same** dc, ch 3;
repeat from ★ 2 times **more**; join with slip st to top of
beginning ch-3.

Rnd 7: Ch 3, dc in next 3 dc, ch 3, skip next ch-3 sp,
work 3-dc Cluster in next ch-2 sp, (ch 2, work
3-dc Cluster in next ch-2 sp) 8 times, ch 3, ★ dc in next
4 dc, ch 3, skip next ch-3 sp, work 3-dc Cluster in next
ch-2 sp, (ch 2, work 3-dc Cluster in next ch-2 sp) 8
times, ch 3; repeat from ★ 2 times **more**; join with
slip st to top of beginning ch-3.

Rnd 8: Ch 3, dc in next 3 dc, ch 4, skip next ch-3 sp,
work 3-dc Cluster in next ch-2 sp, (ch 2, work
3-dc Cluster in next ch-2 sp) 7 times, ch 4, ★ dc in next
4 dc, ch 4, skip next ch-3 sp, work 3-dc Cluster in next
ch-2 sp, (ch 2, work 3-dc Cluster in next ch-2 sp) 7
times, ch 4; repeat from ★ 2 times **more**; join with
slip st to top of beginning ch-3.

Rnd 9: Ch 3, dc in same st, dc in next 2 dc, 2 dc in
next dc, ch 6, skip next ch-4 sp, work 3-dc Cluster in
next ch-2 sp, (ch 2, work 3-dc Cluster in next ch-2 sp) 6
times, ch 6, ★ 2 dc in next dc, dc in next 2 dc, 2 dc in
next dc, ch 6, skip next ch-4 sp, work 3-dc Cluster in
next ch-2 sp, (ch 2, work 3-dc Cluster in next ch-2 sp) 6
times, ch 6; repeat from ★ 2 times **more**; join with
slip st to top of beginning ch-3.

Rnd 10: Ch 4, tr in same st, ★ † tr in next 2 dc, ch 5,
tr in next 2 dc, 2 tr in next dc, ch 6, work 3-dc Cluster
in next ch-2 sp, (ch 2, work 3-dc Cluster in next
ch-2 sp) 5 times, ch 6, † 2 tr in next dc; repeat from
★ 2 times **more**, then repeat from † to † once; join with
slip st to top of beginning ch-4.

Rnd 11: Ch 4, tr in next 3 tr, † ch 3, 7 tr in next loop,
ch 3, tr in next 4 tr, ch 7, work 3-dc Cluster in next
ch-2 sp, (ch 2, work 3-dc Cluster in next ch-2 sp) 4
times, ch 7, tr in next 4 tr, ch 3, 6 tr in next loop, ch 3,
tr in next 4 tr, ch 7, work 3-dc Cluster in next ch-2 sp,
(ch 2, work 3-dc Cluster in next ch-2 sp) 4 times, ch 7 †,
tr in next 4 tr, repeat from † to † once; join with
slip st to top of beginning ch-4.

11

Rnd 12: Ch 4, tr in next 3 tr, † ch 4, 2 tr in next tr, tr in next 5 tr, 2 tr in next tr, ch 4, tr in next 4 tr, ch 8, work 3-dc Cluster in next ch-2 sp, (ch 2, work 3-dc Cluster in next ch-2 sp) 3 times, ch 8, tr in next 4 tr, ch 4, (tr, ch 1, tr) in next tr, ch 1, (tr in next tr, ch 1) 4 times, (tr, ch 1, tr) in next tr, ch 4, tr in next 4 tr, ch 8, work 3-dc Cluster in next ch-2 sp, (ch 2, work 3-dc Cluster in next ch-2 sp) 3 times, ch 8 †, tr in next 4 tr, repeat from † to † once; join with slip st to top of beginning ch-4.

Rnd 13: Ch 4, tr in next 3 tr, † ch 5, tr in next tr, (ch 1, tr in next tr) 8 times, ch 5, tr in next 4 tr, ch 8, work 3-dc Cluster in next ch-2 sp, (ch 2, work 3-dc Cluster in next ch-2 sp) twice, ch 8, tr in next 4 tr, ch 5, tr in next tr, (ch 2, tr in next tr) 7 times, ch 5, tr in next 4 tr, ch 8, work 3-dc Cluster in next ch-2 sp, (ch 2, work 3-dc Cluster in next ch-2 sp) twice, ch 8 †, tr in next 4 tr, repeat from † to † once; join with slip st to top of beginning ch-4.

Rnd 14: Ch 4, tr in next 3 tr, † ch 6, tr in next tr, (ch 2, tr in next tr) 8 times, ch 6, tr in next 4 tr, ch 9, work 3-dc Cluster in next ch-2 sp, ch 2, work 3-dc Cluster in next ch-2 sp, ch 9, tr in next 4 tr, ch 6, tr in next tr, (ch 3, tr in next tr) 7 times, ch 6, tr in next 4 tr, ch 9, work 3-dc Cluster in next ch-2 sp, ch 2, work 3-dc Cluster in next ch-2 sp, ch 9 †, tr in next 4 tr, repeat from † to † once; join with slip st to top of beginning ch-4.

Rnd 15: Ch 4, tr in next 3 tr, † ch 7, work V-St in next tr, ch 3, (tr in next tr, ch 3) 7 times, work V-St in next tr, ch 7, tr in next 4 tr, ch 9, work 3-dc Cluster in next ch-2 sp, ch 9, tr in next 4 tr, ch 7, tr in next tr, (ch 4, tr in next tr) 7 times, ch 7, tr in next 4 tr, ch 9, work 3-dc Cluster in next ch-2 sp, ch 9 †, tr in next 4 tr, repeat from † to † once; join with slip st to top of beginning ch-4.

Rnd 16: Ch 4, tr in next 3 tr, † ch 8, tr in next tr, (ch 4, tr in next tr) 10 times, ch 8, tr in next 4 tr, ch 9, sc in next 3-dc Cluster, ch 9, tr in next 4 tr, ch 7, tr in next tr, (ch 5, tr in next tr) 7 times, ch 7, tr in next 4 tr, ch 9, sc in next 3-dc Cluster, ch 9 †, tr in next 4 tr, repeat from † to † once; join with slip st to top of beginning ch-4.

Rnd 17: Ch 4, tr in next 3 tr, † ch 9, tr in next tr, (ch 5, tr in next tr) 10 times, ch 9, tr in next 4 tr, ch 9, sc in next sc, ch 9, tr in next 4 tr, ch 3, sc in center ch of next loop, (ch 2, 5 tr in next tr, ch 2, sc in center ch of next loop) 8 times, ch 3, tr in next 4 tr, ch 9, sc in next sc, ch 9 †, tr in next 4 tr, repeat from † to † once, join with slip st to top of beginning ch-4.

Rnd 18: Ch 4, tr in next 3 tr, † ch 9, tr in next tr, (ch 5, tr in next tr) 10 times, ch 9, tr in next 4 tr, ch 8, sc in next sc, ch 8, tr in next 4 tr, ch 7, work V-St in center tr of next 5-tr group, (ch 3, work V-St in center tr of next 5-tr group) 7 times, ch 7, tr in next 4 tr, ch 8, sc in next sc, ch 8 †, tr in next 4 tr, repeat from † to † once; join with slip st to top of beginning ch-4.

Rnd 19: Ch 4, tr in next 3 tr, † ch 5, sc in center ch of next loop, ch 3, 5 tr in next tr, (ch 2, sc in center ch of next loop, ch 2, 5 tr in next tr) 10 times, ch 3, sc in center ch of next loop, ch 5, tr in next 4 tr, ch 7, sc in next sc, ch 7, tr in next 4 tr, ch 5, sc in center ch of next loop, ch 3, 7 tr in next V-St (ch-3 sp), (ch 2, sc in center ch of next loop, ch 2, 7 tr in next V-St) 7 times, ch 3, sc in center ch of next loop, ch 5, tr in next 4 tr, ch 7, sc in next sc, ch 7 †, tr in next 4 tr, repeat from † to † once; join with slip st to top of beginning ch-4.

Rnd 20: Ch 4, tr in next 3 tr, † ch 9, work V-St in center tr of next 5-tr group, (ch 3, work V-St in center tr of next 5-tr group) 10 times, ch 9, tr in next 8 tr, ch 7, work V-St in center tr of next 7-tr group, (ch 5, work V-St in center tr of next 7-tr group) 7 times, ch 7 †, tr in next 8 tr, repeat from † to † once, tr in next 4 tr; join with slip st to top of beginning ch-4.

Rnd 21: Ch 3, [YO twice, insert hook in **next** tr, YO and pull up a loop, (YO and draw through 2 loops on hook) twice] 3 times, YO and draw through all 4 loops on hook, † ch 5, sc in center ch of next loop, ch 4, 7 tr in next V-St, (ch 2, sc in center ch of next loop, ch 2, 7 tr in next V-St) 10 times, ch 4, sc in center ch of next loop, ch 5, work 4-tr Cluster, ch 1, work 4-tr Cluster, place marker in ch-1 sp just made to mark Side placement, ch 5, sc in center ch of next loop, ch 3, (4 tr, work Picot, 3 tr) in next V-St, [ch 3, sc in center ch of next loop, ch 3, (4 tr, work Picot, 3 tr) in next V-St] 7 times, ch 3, sc in center ch of next loop, ch 5, work 4-tr Cluster, ch 1 †, work 4-tr Cluster, repeat from † to † once; join with slip st to first st, finish off.

SIDE

Row 1: With **wrong** side facing, join thread with slip st in first marked ch-1 sp; ch 1, sc in same sp, ch 9, work V-St in center tr of next 7-tr group, (ch 5, work V-St in center tr of next 7-tr group) 10 times, ch 9, sc in next ch-1 sp (between 4-tr Clusters).

Row 2: Ch 9, turn; 7 tr in next V-St, (ch 3, sc in center ch of next loop, ch 3, 7 tr in next V-St) 10 times, ch 9, slip st in last sc.

Row 3: Ch 10, turn; work V-St in center tr of next 7-tr group, (ch 7, work V-St in center tr of next 7-tr group) 10 times, ch 10, slip st in last st.

Row 4: Ch 11, turn; 7 tr in next V-St, (ch 3, sc in center ch of next loop, ch 3, 7 tr in next V-St) 10 times, ch 11, slip st in last st.

Row 5: Ch 13, turn; work V-St in center tr of next 7-tr group, (ch 9, work V-St in center tr of next 7-tr group) 10 times, ch 13, slip st in last st.

Row 6: Ch 14, turn; (5 tr, work Picot, 4 tr) in next V-St, ★ ch 4, sc in center ch of next loop, ch 4, (5 tr, work Picot, 4 tr) in next V-St; repeat from ★ 9 times **more**, ch 14, slip st in last st; finish off.

Joining in next marked ch-1 sp, repeat for second side.

June

Finished Size: Approximately 11″ x 11″

MATERIALS

Bedspread Weight Cotton Thread (size 10),
  approximately 185 yards
Steel crochet hook, size 6 (1.50 mm) **or** size needed
  for gauge

GAUGE: Rnds 1-5 = 2¾″

PATTERN STITCHES

Beginning Cluster: Ch 2, ★ (YO, insert hook in **next** dc, YO and pull up a loop, YO and draw through 2 loops on hook; repeat from ★ once **more**, YO and draw through all 3 loops on hook.

Cluster: YO, insert hook in **same** dc, YO and pull up a loop, YO and draw through 2 loops on hook, ★ YO, insert hook in **next** dc, YO and pull up a loop, YO and draw through 2 loops on hook; repeat from ★ once **more**, YO and draw through all 4 loops on hook.

Treble Crochet (abbreviated tr): YO twice, insert hook in stitch indicated, YO and pull up a loop (4 loops on hook), (YO and draw through 2 loops on hook) 3 times.

Beginning Shell: Ch 3, (dc, ch 3, 2 dc) in same stitch or space.

Shell: (2 Dc, ch 3, 2 dc) in stitch or space indicated.

Picot: Slip st in third ch from hook.

Double Treble Crochet (abbreviated dtr): YO 3 times, insert hook in stitch indicated, YO and pull up a loop (5 loops on hook), (YO and draw through 2 loops on hook) 4 times.

Ch 8, join with slip st to form a ring.

Rnd 1 (Right side): Ch 3, 15 dc in ring; join with slip st to top of beginning ch-3: 16 sts.

Note: Loop a short piece of thread around any stitch to mark last round as **right** side.

Rnd 2: Work beginning Cluster, ch 5, (work Cluster, ch 5) around, working last Cluster in first st; join with slip st to beginning Cluster: 8 loops.

Rnd 3: Slip st in first loop, ch 1, work (sc, hdc, 5 dc, hdc, sc) in same loop and in each loop around; join with slip st to first sc.

Rnd 4: Working in Back Loop Only of each Cluster on Rnd 2, slip st in first Cluster, ch 1, sc in same st, (ch 7, sc in next Cluster) around, ch 3, tr in first sc to form last loop.

Rnd 5: Ch 3, (3 dc, hdc, sc) in same loop, (sc, hdc, 7 dc, hdc, sc) in each loop around, (sc, hdc, 3 dc) in first loop; join with slip st to top of beginning ch-3: 8 Petals.

Rnd 6: Ch 1, sc in same st, ch 11, (sc in center dc of next Petal, ch 11) around; join with slip st to first sc.

Rnd 7: Slip st in next 2 chs, ch 1, sc in same st, (ch 3, skip next ch, sc in next ch) 4 times, ★ ch 3, skip next sc and next ch, sc in next ch, (ch 3, skip next ch, sc in next ch) 4 times; repeat from ★ around, ch 1, hdc in first sc to form last sp.

13

Rnd 8: Ch 6, dc in same sp, ch 2, sc in next ch-3 sp, (ch 3, sc in next ch-3 sp) 8 times, ch 2, ★ (dc, ch 3, dc) in next ch-3 sp, ch 2, sc in next ch-3 sp, (ch 3, sc in next ch-3 sp) 8 times, ch 2; repeat from ★ around; join with slip st to third ch of beginning ch-6.

Rnd 9: Slip st in first sp, work beginning Shell, ch 3, skip next ch-2 sp, (sc in next ch-3 sp, ch 3) 8 times, skip next ch-2 sp, ★ work Shell in next ch-3 sp, ch 3, skip next ch-2 sp, (sc in next ch-3 sp, ch 3) 8 times, skip next ch-2 sp; repeat from ★ around; join with slip st to top of beginning ch-3.

Rnd 10: Slip st in next dc and in first ch-3 sp, work (beginning Shell, ch 3, Shell) in same sp, ch 3, skip next ch-3 sp, (sc in next ch-3 sp, ch 3) 7 times, ★ work (Shell, ch 3, Shell) in next Shell (ch-3 sp), ch 3, skip next ch-3 sp, (sc in next ch-3 sp, ch 3) 7 times; repeat from ★ around; join with slip st to top of beginning ch-3.

Rnd 11: Slip st in next dc and in first ch-3 sp, work beginning Shell, ch 1, ★ † dc in next ch-3 sp, (ch 3, dc in **same** sp) twice, ch 1, work Shell in next Shell, ch 3, skip next ch-3 sp, (sc in next ch-3 sp, ch 3) 6 times †, work Shell in next Shell, ch 1; repeat from ★ 2 times **more**, then repeat from † to † once; join with slip st to top of beginning ch-3.

Rnd 12: Slip st in next dc and in first ch-3 sp, work beginning Shell, ★ † (ch 1, work Shell in next ch-3 sp) 3 times, ch 3, skip next ch-3 sp, (sc in next ch-3 sp, ch 3) 5 times †, work Shell in next Shell; repeat from ★ 2 times **more**, then repeat from † to † once; join with slip st to top of beginning ch-3.

Rnd 13: Slip st in next dc and in first ch-3 sp, work beginning Shell, ★ † ch 1, work Shell in next Shell, ch 8, work Shell in next Shell, ch 1, work Shell in next Shell, ch 4, skip next ch-3 sp, sc in next ch-3 sp, (ch 3, sc in next ch-3 sp) 3 times, ch 4 †, work Shell in next Shell; repeat from ★ 2 times **more**, then repeat from † to † once; join with slip st to top of beginning ch-3.

Rnd 14: Slip st in next dc and in first ch-3 sp, work beginning Shell, ★ † ch 2, work Shell in next Shell, ch 3, 8 sc in next loop, ch 3, work Shell in next Shell, ch 2, work Shell in next Shell, ch 5, skip next loop, sc in next ch-3 sp, (ch 3, sc in next ch-3 sp) twice, ch 5 †, work Shell in next Shell; repeat from ★ 2 times **more**, then repeat from † to † once; join with slip st to top of beginning ch-3.

Rnd 15: Slip st in next dc and in first ch-3 sp, work beginning Shell, ★ † ch 2, work Shell in next Shell, ch 3, 2 dc in next sc, dc in next 6 sc, 2 dc in next sc, **turn**, slip st in first dc, ch 5, (skip next 2 dc, sc in next dc, ch 5) twice, skip next 2 dc, slip st in next dc, **turn**, slip st in first loop, (sc, hdc, 3 dc, hdc, sc) in same loop and in next 2 loops, slip st in next st, ch 3, work Shell in next Shell, ch 2, work Shell in next Shell, ch 7, skip next loop, sc in next ch-3 sp, ch 3, sc in next ch-3 sp, ch 7 †, work Shell in next Shell; repeat from ★ 2 times **more**, then repeat from † to † once; join with slip st to top of beginning ch-3.

Rnd 16: Slip st in next dc and in first ch-3 sp, ch 3, dc in same sp, ★ † ch 4, work Picot, ch 3, work Picot, ch 1, 2 dc in same sp, ch 3, 2 dc in next Shell, ch 4, work Picot, ch 3, work Picot, ch 1, 2 dc in same sp, ch 6, (work Picot, ch 3) twice, skip next ch-3 sp, sc in next sc, ch 7, work Picot, ch 3, work Picot, ch 5, sc in sp between Petals, ch 10, work Picot, ch 3, work Picot, ch 8, sc in next sp between Petals, ch 7, work Picot, ch 3, work Picot, ch 5, sc in last sc of next Petal, ch 6, (work Picot, ch 3) twice, 2 dc in next Shell, ch 4, work Picot, ch 3, work Picot, ch 1, 2 dc in same sp, ch 3, 2 dc in next Shell, ch 4, work Picot, ch 3, work Picot, ch 1, 2 dc in same sp, ch 7, skip next loop, (sc, ch 3, work Picot, sc) in next ch-3 sp, ch 7 †, 2 dc in next Shell; repeat from ★ 2 times **more**, then repeat from † to † once; join with slip st to top of beginning ch-3, finish off.

Rnd 17: With **right** side facing, join thread with slip st in ch between Picots of any corner loop; ch 16, ★ † tr in ch between Picots of next loop, ch 7, tr in ch between Picots of next loop, ch 5, tr in ch between Picots of next loop, ch 7, tr in ch between Picots of next loop, ch 9, tr in ch between Picots of next loop, ch 7, tr in ch between Picots of next loop, ch 5, tr in ch between Picots of next loop, ch 7, tr in ch between Picots of next loop, ch 11 †, dtr in ch between Picots of next loop, ch 11; repeat from ★ 2 times **more**, then repeat from † to † once; join with slip st to fifth ch of beginning ch-16: 36 loops.

Rnd 18: Ch 3, ★ dc in each ch and in each tr across to next corner dtr, (dc, ch 3, dc) in corner dtr; repeat from ★ 2 times **more**, dc in each ch and in each tr across, dc in same st as beginning ch-3, ch 1, hdc in top of beginning ch-3 to form last sp.

Rnd 19: Work (beginning Shell, ch 3, 2 dc) in same st, ★ † ch 3, skip next 3 dc, sc in next dc, ch 3, (skip next 5 dc, work Shell in next dc, ch 3, skip next 5 dc, sc in next dc, ch 3) 6 times †, work (Shell, ch 3, 2 dc) in center ch of next loop; repeat from ★ 2 times **more**, then repeat from † to † once; join with slip st to top of beginning ch-3.

Rnd 20: Slip st in next dc and in first ch-3 sp, work beginning Shell, ★ † ch 2, work Shell in next ch-3 sp, ch 3, sc in next sc, ch 3, (work Shell in next Shell, ch 3, sc in next sc, ch 3) 6 times †, work Shell in next ch-3 sp; repeat from ★ 2 times **more**, then repeat from † to † once; join with slip st to top of beginning ch-3.

Rnd 21: Slip st in next dc and in first ch-3 sp, work beginning Shell, ★ † ch 3, sc in next ch-2 sp, ch 3, (work Shell in next Shell, ch 4, sc in next sc, ch 4) 7 times †, work Shell in next Shell; repeat from ★ 2 times **more**, then repeat from † to † once; join with slip st to top of beginning ch-3.

Rnd 22: Ch 1, sc in same st and in next dc, ★ † (sc, ch 4, slip st in sc just made, sc) in next ch-3 sp, sc in next 2 dc, 3 sc in next ch-3 sp, sc in next sc, ch 3, slip st in sc just made, 3 sc in next ch-3 sp, [sc in next 2 dc, (sc, ch 4, slip st in sc just made, sc) in next ch-3 sp, sc in next 2 dc, 4 sc in next ch-4 sp, sc in next sc, 4 sc in next ch-4 sp] 7 times †, sc in next 2 dc; repeat from ★ 2 times **more**, then repeat from † to † once; join with slip st to first sc, finish off.

Finished Size: Approximately 14½" in diameter

MATERIALS
Bedspread Weight Cotton Thread (size 10), approximately 125 yards
Steel crochet hook, size 6 (1.50 mm) **or** size needed for gauge

GAUGE: Rnds 1-6 = 4"

PATTERN STITCHES
Treble Crochet (abbreviated tr): YO twice, insert hook in stitch indicated, YO and pull up a loop (4 loops on hook), (YO and draw through 2 loops on hook) 3 times.

Beginning Cluster: Ch 3, ★ YO twice, insert hook in **same** space and pull up a loop, (YO and draw through 2 loops on hook) twice; repeat from ★ once **more**, YO and draw through all 3 loops on hook.

Cluster: ★ YO twice, insert hook in space indicated and pull up a loop, (YO and draw through 2 loops on hook) twice; repeat from ★ 2 times **more**, YO and draw through all 4 loops on hook.

Beginning Picot Shell: Ch 4, (tr, ch 4, slip st in fourth ch from hook, ch 1, 2 tr) in stitch indicated.

Picot Shell: (2 Tr, ch 4, slip st in fourth ch from hook, ch 1, 2 tr) in stitch indicated.

Beginning Shell: Ch 3, (dc, ch 2, 2 dc) in stitch or space indicated.

Shell: (2 Dc, ch 2, 2 dc) in stitch or space indicated.

Ch 8, join with slip st to form a ring.

Rnd 1 (Right side): Ch 3, 15 dc in ring; join with slip st to top of beginning ch-3: 16 sts.

Rnd 2: Ch 9, (tr in next dc, ch 5) around; join with slip st to fourth ch of beginning ch-9: 16 loops.

Rnd 3: Ch 3, sc in first loop, ★ (dc, ch 3, dc) in next tr, sc in next loop; repeat from ★ around; dc in same st as beginning ch-3, ch 1, hdc in top of beginning ch-3 to form last sp.

Rnd 4: Ch 1, sc in same sp, ch 5, (sc in next ch-3 sp, ch 5) around; join with slip st to first sc.

Rnd 5: Ch 3, sc in first loop, ★ (dc, ch 5, dc) in next sc, sc in next loop; repeat from ★ around, dc in same st as beginning ch-3, ch 2, dc in top of beginning ch-3 to form last loop.

Rnd 6: Work beginning Cluster, ch 3, (sc, ch 3, sc) in center ch of next loop, ch 3, ★ work (Cluster, ch 5, Cluster) in next loop, ch 3, (sc, ch 3, sc) in center ch of next loop, ch 3; repeat from ★ around, work Cluster in first loop, ch 2, dc in top of beginning Cluster to form last loop.

Rnd 7: Ch 21, (skip next 2 Clusters, tr in center ch of next ch-5 loop, ch 17) around; join with slip st to fourth ch of beginning ch-21: 8 loops.

Rnd 8: Work beginning Picot Shell in same st, (ch 3, skip next 5 chs, work Picot Shell in next ch) twice, ★ ch 3, skip next 5 chs, work Picot Shell in next tr, (ch 3, skip next 5 chs, work Picot Shell in next ch) twice; repeat from ★ around, ch 1, hdc in top of beginning ch-4 to form last sp: 24 Picot Shells.

Rnds 9 and 10: Work beginning Picot Shell in same st, (ch 3, work Picot Shell in center ch of next ch-3 sp) around, ch 1, hdc in top of beginning ch-4 to form last loop.

Rnds 11 and 12: Work beginning Picot Shell in same st, (ch 5, work Picot Shell in center ch of next loop) around, ch 2, dc in top of beginning ch-4 to form last loop.

Rnd 13: Ch 16, (tr in center ch of next loop, ch 12) around; join with slip st to fourth ch of beginning ch-16: 24 loops.

Rnd 14: Slip st in first loop, ch 3, 14 dc in same loop, 15 dc in each loop around; join with slip st to top of beginning ch-3: 360 sts.

Rnd 15: Slip st in next dc, ch 1, sc in same dc, (ch 3, skip next 2 dc, sc in next dc) around, ch 1, hdc in first sc to form last sp: 120 sps.

Rnd 16: Work beginning Shell in same st, ch 2, sc in next ch-3 sp, (ch 3, sc in next ch-3 sp) 3 times, ch 2, ★ work Shell in center ch of next ch-3 sp, ch 2, sc in next ch-3 sp, (ch 3, sc in next ch-3 sp) 3 times, ch 2; repeat from ★ around; join with slip st to top of beginning ch-3: 24 Shells.

Rnd 17: Slip st in next dc and in first ch-2 sp, work beginning Shell in same sp, ch 4, skip next ch-2 sp, sc in next ch-3 sp, (ch 3, sc in next ch-3 sp) twice, ch 4, ★ work Shell in next Shell (ch-2 sp), ch 4, skip next ch-2 sp, sc in next ch-3 sp, (ch 3, sc in next ch-3 sp) twice, ch 4; repeat from ★ around; join with slip st to top of beginning ch-3.

Rnd 18: Slip st in next dc and in first ch-2 sp, work beginning Shell in same sp, ch 6, skip next ch-4 sp, sc in next ch-3 sp, ch 3, sc in next ch-3 sp, ch 6, ★ work Shell in next Shell, ch 6, skip next ch-4 sp, sc in next ch-3 sp, ch 3, sc in next ch-3 sp, ch 6; repeat from ★ around; join with slip st to top of beginning ch-3.

Rnd 19: Slip st in next dc and in first ch-2 sp, ch 3, (3 dc, ch 4, slip st in fourth ch from hook, ch 1, 4 dc) in same sp, ch 7, skip next loop, (sc, ch 3, sc) in center ch of next ch-3 sp, ch 7, ★ (4 dc, ch 4, slip st in fourth ch from hook, ch 1, 4 dc) in next Shell, ch 7, skip next loop, (sc, ch 3, sc) in center ch of next ch-3 sp, ch 7; repeat from ★ around; join with slip st to top of beginning ch-3, finish off.

Finished Size: Approximately 13″ in diameter

MATERIALS

Bedspread Weight Cotton Thread (size 10), approximately 175 yards

Steel crochet hook, size 6 (1.50 mm) **or** size needed for gauge

GAUGE: Rnds 1-3 = 2″

PATTERN STITCHES

Treble Crochet (abbreviated tr): YO twice, insert hook in stitch or space indicated, YO and pull up a loop (4 loops on hook), (YO and draw through 2 loops on hook) 3 times.

Picot: Ch 3, slip st in stitch just made.

Double Treble Crochet (abbreviated dtr): YO 3 times, insert hook in stitch indicated, YO and pull up a loop (5 loops on hook), (YO and draw through 2 loops on hook) 4 times.

Shell: † YO twice, insert hook in **next** dc, YO and pull up a loop, (YO and draw through 2 loops on hook) twice, YO twice, insert hook in **same** dc, YO and pull up a loop, (YO and draw through 2 loops on hook) twice, YO and draw through all 3 loops on hook †, ch 2, repeat from † to † once.

V-St: (Tr, ch 2, tr) in dc indicated.

Ch 8, join with slip st to form a ring.

Rnd 1 (Right side): Ch 3, 15 dc in ring; join with slip st to top of beginning ch-3: 16 sts.

Rnd 2: Ch 6, (tr in next dc, ch 2) around; join with slip st to fourth ch of beginning ch-6: 16 ch-2 sps.

Rnd 3: Ch 6, dc in next tr, ch 4, slip st in third ch from hook, ch 1, ★ dc in next tr, ch 3, dc in next tr, ch 4, slip st in third ch from hook, ch 1; repeat from ★ around; join with slip st to third ch of beginning ch-6.

Rnd 4: Slip st in first ch-3 sp, ch 4, (tr, work Picot, 2 tr) in same sp, ★ ch 10, skip next sp, (2 tr, work Picot, 2 tr) in next ch-3 sp; repeat from ★ around, ch 5, dtr in top of beginning ch-4 to form last loop: 8 loops.

Rnd 5: Ch 3, 6 dc in same loop, ch 2, (13 dc in next loop, ch 2) around, 6 dc in first loop; join with slip st to top of beginning ch-3.

Rnd 6: Ch 6, tr in same st, ch 3, skip next 3 dc, work Shell, skip next ch-2 sp and next dc, work Shell, ch 3, ★ skip next 3 dc, work V-St in next dc, ch 3, skip next 3 dc, work Shell, skip next ch-2 sp and next dc, work Shell, ch 3; repeat from ★ around; join with slip st to fourth ch of beginning ch-6: 16 Shells.

Rnd 7: Slip st in first ch-2 sp, ch 4, 8 tr in same sp, ch 3, [sc in next Shell (ch-2 sp), ch 3] twice, ★ skip next ch-3 sp, 9 tr in next V-St (ch-2 sp), ch 3, (sc in next Shell, ch 3) twice; repeat from ★ around; join with slip st to top of beginning ch-4.

Rnd 8: Ch 5, tr in next tr, (ch 1, tr in next tr) 7 times, ch 4, skip next ch-3 sp, (sc, ch 3, sc) in next ch-3 sp, ch 4, ★ tr in next tr, (ch 1, tr in next tr) 8 times, ch 4, skip next ch-3 sp, (sc, ch 3, sc) in next ch-3 sp, ch 4; repeat from ★ around; join with slip st to fourth ch of beginning ch-5.

Rnd 9: Slip st in first ch-1 sp, ch 1, sc in same sp, (ch 3, sc in next ch-1 sp) 7 times, ★ ch 7, skip next 3 sps, sc in next ch-1 sp, (ch 3, sc in next ch-1 sp) 7 times; repeat from ★ around, ch 2, dtr in first sc to form last loop.

Rnd 10: Ch 1, (sc, ch 7) twice in same loop, sc in next ch-3 sp, (ch 7, skip next ch-3 sp, sc in next ch-3 sp) 3 times, ★ ch 7, (sc, ch 7) twice in next loop, sc in next ch-3 sp, (ch 7, skip next ch-3 sp, sc in next ch-3 sp) 3 times; repeat from ★ around, ch 3, tr in first sc to form last loop: 48 loops.

Rnd 11: Ch 1, sc in same loop, (ch 7, sc in next loop) around, ch 3, tr in first sc to form last loop.

Rnd 12: Ch 1, sc in same loop, ch 7, sc in next loop, ch 7, slip st in fourth ch from hook, ch 3, sc in next loop, ★ (ch 7, sc in next loop) twice, ch 7, slip st in fourth ch from hook, ch 3, sc in next loop; repeat from ★ around, ch 2, dtr in first sc to form last loop.

Rnd 13: Ch 4, 3 tr in same loop, ch 5, 4 tr in next loop, ★ ch 10, skip next loop, 4 tr in next ch-7 loop, ch 5, 4 tr in next loop; repeat from ★ around, ch 5, dtr in top of beginning ch-4 to form last loop.

Rnd 14: Ch 3, 6 dc in same loop, ch 5, (sc, ch 3, sc) in center ch of next loop, ch 5, ★ 13 dc in next loop, ch 5, (sc, ch 3, sc) in center ch of next loop, ch 5; repeat from ★ around, 6 dc in first loop; join with slip st to top of beginning ch-3.

Rnd 15: Ch 6, tr in same st, ch 3, skip next 3 dc, work Shell, ch 5, skip next 2 ch-5 sps and next dc, work Shell, ch 3, skip next 3 dc, ★ work V-St in next dc, ch 3, skip next 3 dc, work Shell, ch 5, skip next 2 ch-5 sps and next dc, work Shell, ch 3, skip next 3 dc; repeat from ★ around; join with slip st to fourth ch of beginning ch-6: 32 Shells.

Rnd 16: Slip st in first sp, ch 4, 8 tr in same sp, ★ † ch 3, sc in next Shell, ch 4, sc in center ch of next loop, ch 4, sc in next Shell, ch 3 †, 9 tr in next V-St; repeat from ★ 14 times **more**, then repeat from † to † once; join with slip st to top of beginning ch-4.

Rnd 17: Ch 5, tr in next tr, (ch 1, tr in next tr) 7 times, ch 6, skip next sc, hdc in next sc, ch 6, ★ tr in next tr, (ch 1, tr in next tr) 8 times, ch 6, skip next sc, hdc in next sc, ch 6; repeat from ★ around; join with slip st to fourth ch of beginning ch-5.

Rnd 18: Ch 6, tr in next tr, (ch 2, tr in next tr) 7 times, ch 5, sc in next hdc, ch 5, ★ tr in next tr, (ch 2, tr in next tr) 8 times, ch 5, sc in next hdc, ch 5; repeat from ★ around; join with slip st to fourth ch of beginning ch-6.

Rnd 19: Ch 1, sc in same st, ★ † [(sc, ch 3, sc) in next ch-2 sp, sc in next tr] 8 times, 5 sc in each of next 2 loops †, sc in next tr; repeat from ★ 14 times **more**, then repeat from † to † once; join with slip st to first sc, finish off.

September

Finished Size: Approximately 15" x 20"

MATERIALS

Bedspread Weight Cotton Thread (size 10),
approximately 1 ball plus 45 yards
(282 yards per ball)
Steel crochet hook, size 6 (1.50 mm) **or** size needed
for gauge

GAUGE: Each Motif = 2¼"

PATTERN STITCHES

Beginning Cluster: Ch 3, ★ YO twice, insert hook in **same** space and pull up a loop, (YO and draw through 2 loops on hook) twice; repeat from ★ once **more**, YO and draw through all 3 loops on hook.

Cluster: ★ YO twice, insert hook in space indicated and pull up a loop, (YO and draw through 2 loops on hook) twice; repeat from ★ 2 times **more**, YO and draw through all 4 loops on hook.

Treble Crochet (abbreviated tr): YO twice, insert hook in stitch or space indicated, YO and pull up a loop (4 loops on hook), (YO and draw through 2 loops on hook) 3 times.

Beginning Shell: Ch 3, (2 dc, ch 3, 3 dc) in same stitch or space.

Shell: (3 Dc, ch 3, 3 dc) in stitch or space indicated.

Dtr Cluster: YO 3 times, insert hook in **same** stitch or space, YO and pull up a loop, (YO and draw through 2 loops on hook) 3 times, YO 3 times, insert hook in **next** stitch or space, YO and pull up a loop, (YO and draw through 2 loops on hook) 3 times, YO and draw through all 3 loops on hook.

Double Treble Crochet (abbreviated dtr): YO 3 times, insert hook in stitch or space indicated, YO and pull up a loop (5 loops on hook), (YO and draw through 2 loops on hook) 4 times.

FIRST MOTIF

Ch 8, join with slip st to form a ring.

Rnd 1 (Right side): Ch 1, 12 sc in ring; join with slip st to first sc.

Note: Loop a short piece of thread around any stitch to mark last round as **right** side.

Rnd 2: Ch 5, (dc in next sc, ch 2) around; join with slip st to third ch of beginning ch-5: 12 ch-2 sps.

Rnd 3: Slip st in first sp, ch 1, sc in same sp, ch 3, (sc in next ch-2 sp, ch 3) around; join with slip st to first sc.

Rnd 4: Slip st in first sp, work beginning Cluster, ch 5, (work Cluster in next ch-3 sp, ch 5) around; join with slip st to beginning Cluster, finish off.

SECOND MOTIF

Work same as First Motif through Rnd 3.

Rnd 4 (Joining rnd): Slip st in first sp, work beginning Cluster, (ch 5, work Cluster in next ch-3 sp) 9 times, ch 2, holding **First Motif** with **right** side facing, slip st in center ch of any ch-5 on **First Motif**, ch 2, work Cluster in next ch-3 sp on **Second Motif**, ch 2, slip st in center ch of next ch-5 on **First Motif**, ch 2, work Cluster in next ch-3 sp on **Second Motif**, ch 5; join with slip st to beginning Cluster, finish off.

Work **Third Motif** in same manner, skipping next 4 loops on **Second Motif** when joining; do **not** finish off.

BORDER

Rnd 1: Slip st in next 3 chs, ch 6, dc in same ch, ch 3, (dc, ch 3) twice in center ch of next 7 loops, † (tr, ch 3) twice in center ch of next loop, skip joining, (tr, ch 3) twice in center ch of next loop, (dc, ch 3) twice in center ch of next 2 loops, (tr, ch 3) twice in center ch of next loop, skip joining, (tr, ch 3) twice in center ch of next loop †, (dc, ch 3) twice in center ch of next 8 loops, repeat from † to † once; join with slip st to third ch of beginning ch-6.

Rnd 2: Slip st in first sp, work beginning Shell, skip next ch-3 sp, (work Shell in next ch-3 sp, skip next ch-3 sp) around; join with slip st to top of beginning ch-3.

Rnd 3: Slip st in next 2 dc and in first sp, work beginning Shell, ch 1, [work Shell in next Shell (ch-3 sp), ch 1] 6 times, work Shell in next 8 Shells, ch 1, (work Shell in next Shell, ch 1) 6 times, work Shell in last 7 Shells; join with slip st to top of beginning ch-3.

Rnd 4: Slip st in next 2 dc and in first sp, ch 1, sc in same sp, ch 6, working in each Shell, work dtr Cluster, (ch 6, sc in same sp, ch 6, work dtr Cluster) around, working last dtr Cluster in same sp as first sc, dtr in same sp.

Rnd 5: Ch 1, sc in same st, ch 6, working in each dtr Cluster, work dtr Cluster, (ch 6, sc in same st, ch 6, work dtr Cluster) around, working last dtr Cluster in same st as first sc, dtr in same st.

Rnd 6: Work beginning Shell, ch 4, (work Shell in next dtr Cluster, ch 4) 9 times, work Shell in next 4 dtr Clusters, ch 4, (work Shell in next dtr Cluster, ch 4) 10 times, work Shell in next 4 dtr Clusters, ch 4; join with slip st to top of beginning ch-3.

Rnd 7: Slip st in next 2 dc and in first sp, work beginning Shell, ch 4, (work Shell in next Shell, ch 4) 9 times, work Shell in next 4 Shells, ch 4, (work Shell in next Shell, ch 4) 10 times, work Shell in next 4 Shells, ch 4; join with slip st to top of beginning ch-3.

Rnd 8: Slip st in next 2 dc and in first sp, work beginning Shell, ch 5, work Shell in next Shell, † ch 9, ★ work Shell in next Shell, (ch 5, work Shell in next Shell) twice, ch 9; repeat from ★ once **more**, (work Shell in next Shell, ch 5) twice, work Shell in next 4 Shells †, (ch 5, work Shell in next Shell) twice, repeat from † to † once, ch 5; join with slip st to top of beginning ch-3.

Rnd 9: Slip st in next 2 dc and in first sp, work beginning Shell, ch 5, work Shell in next Shell, † ch 3, 9 tr in next loop, ch 3, ★ work Shell in next Shell, (ch 5, work Shell in next Shell) twice, ch 3, 9 tr in next loop, ch 3; repeat from ★ once **more**, (work Shell in next Shell, ch 5) twice, work Shell in next 4 Shells †, (ch 5, work Shell in next Shell) twice, repeat from † to † once, ch 5; join with slip st to top of beginning ch-3.

Rnd 10: Slip st in next 2 dc and in first sp, work beginning Shell, ch 5, work Shell in next Shell, † ch 3, tr in next tr, (ch 1, tr in next tr) 8 times, ch 3, ★ work Shell in next Shell, (ch 5, work Shell in next Shell) twice, ch 3, tr in next tr, (ch 1, tr in next tr) 8 times, ch 3; repeat from ★ once **more**, (work Shell in next Shell, ch 5) twice, work Shell in next 4 Shells †, (ch 5, work Shell in next Shell) twice, repeat from † to † once, ch 5; join with slip st to top of beginning ch-3.

Rnd 11: Slip st in next 2 dc and in first sp, work beginning Shell, ch 6, work Shell in next Shell, † ch 4, skip next loop, sc in next ch-1 sp, (ch 3, sc in next ch-1 sp) 7 times, ch 4, ★ work Shell in next Shell, (ch 6, work Shell in next Shell) twice, ch 4, skip next loop, sc in next ch-1 sp, (ch 3, sc in next ch-1 sp) 7 times, ch 4; repeat from ★ once **more**, (work Shell in next Shell, ch 6) twice, work Shell in next 4 Shells †, (ch 6, work Shell in next Shell) twice, repeat from † to † once, ch 6; join with slip st to top of beginning ch-3.

Continued on page 21.

Rnd 12: Slip st in next 2 dc and in first sp, work beginning Shell, ch 6, work Shell in next Shell, † ch 4, skip next loop, sc in next ch-3 sp, (ch 3, sc in next ch-3 sp) 6 times, ch 4, ★ work Shell in next Shell, (ch 6, work Shell in next Shell) twice, ch 4, skip next loop, sc in next ch-3 sp, (ch 3, sc in next ch-3 sp) 6 times, ch 4; repeat from ★ once **more**, (work Shell in next Shell, ch 6) twice, work Shell in next 4 Shells †, (ch 6, work Shell in next Shell) twice, repeat from † to † once, ch 6; join with slip st to top of beginning ch-3.

Rnd 13: Slip st in next 2 dc and in first sp, work beginning Shell, ★ † ch 6, work (Shell, ch 3, 3 dc) in next Shell, ch 4, skip next loop, sc in next ch-3 sp, (ch 3, sc in next ch-3 sp) 5 times, ch 4, work (Shell, ch 3, 3 dc) in next Shell, ch 6, work Shell in next Shell; repeat from ★ 2 times **more**, ch 6, work Shell in next 4 Shells, ch 6 †, work Shell in next Shell, repeat from † to † once; join with slip st to top of beginning ch-3.

Rnd 14: Slip st in next 2 dc and in first sp, work beginning Shell, ★ † ch 6, work Shell in each of next 2 ch-3 sps, ch 4, skip next loop, sc in next ch-3 sp, (ch 3, sc in next ch-3 sp) 4 times, ch 4, work Shell in each of next 2 ch-3 sps, ch 6, work Shell in next Shell; repeat from ★ 2 times **more**, ch 6, work Shell in next 4 Shells, ch 6 †, work Shell in next Shell, repeat from † to † once; join with slip st to top of beginning ch-3.

Rnd 15: Slip st in next 2 dc and in first sp, work beginning Shell, ch 7, ★ work Shell in next Shell, † ch 3, work Shell in next Shell, ch 4, skip next loop, sc in next ch-3 sp, (ch 3, sc in next ch-3 sp) 3 times, ch 4, work Shell in next Shell, ch 3, (work Shell in next Shell, ch 7) twice; repeat from ★ 2 times **more**, work Shell in next 4 Shells †, (ch 7, work Shell in next Shell) twice, repeat from † to † once, ch 7; join with slip st to top of beginning ch-3.

Rnd 16: Slip st in next 2 dc and in first sp, work beginning Shell, ch 7, ★ work Shell in next Shell, † ch 2, (dc, ch 3, dc) in center ch of next loop, ch 2, work Shell in next Shell, ch 4, skip next loop, sc in next ch-3 sp, (ch 3, sc in next ch-3 sp) twice, ch 4, work Shell in next Shell, ch 2, (dc, ch 3, dc) in center ch of next loop, ch 2, (work Shell in next Shell, ch 7) twice; repeat from ★ 2 times **more**, work Shell in next 4 Shells †, (ch 7, work Shell in next Shell) twice, repeat from † to † once, ch 7; join with slip st to top of beginning ch-3.

Rnd 17: Slip st in next 2 dc and in first sp, work beginning Shell, ch 7, ★ work Shell in next Shell, † ch 3, skip next ch-2 sp, dc in next dc, 5 dc in next ch-3 sp, dc in next dc, ch 3, work Shell in next Shell, ch 5, skip next loop, sc in next ch-3 sp, ch 3, sc in next ch-3 sp, ch 5, work Shell in next Shell, ch 3, skip next ch-2 sp, dc in next dc, 5 dc in next ch-3 sp, dc in next dc, ch 3, (work Shell in next Shell, ch 7) twice; repeat from ★ 2 times **more**, work Shell in next 4 Shells †, (ch 7, work Shell in next Shell) twice, repeat from † to † once, ch 7; join with slip st to top of beginning ch-3.

Note: Work Picot as follows: Ch 3, slip st in stitch just made.

Rnd 18: Slip st in next 2 dc and in first sp, work beginning Shell, ch 7, ★ work Shell in next Shell, † ch 4, sc in next dc, work Picot, sc in next 5 dc, work Picot, sc in next dc, ch 4, work Shell in next Shell, ch 6, skip next loop, sc in next ch-3 sp, ch 6, work Shell in next Shell, ch 4, sc in next dc, work Picot, sc in next 5 dc, work Picot, sc in next dc, ch 4, (work Shell in next Shell, ch 7) twice; repeat from ★ 2 times **more**, work Shell in next 4 Shells †, (ch 7, work Shell in next Shell) twice, repeat from † to † once, ch 7; join with slip st to top of beginning ch-3.

Rnd 19: Slip st in next 2 dc and in first sp, work beginning Shell, † ch 7, ★ work (Shell, ch 3, 3 dc) in next Shell, ch 5, skip next Picot and next sc, dc in next 3 sc, ch 5, work (Shell, ch 3, 3 dc) in each of next 2 Shells, ch 5, skip next Picot and next sc, dc in next 3 sc, ch 5, work (Shell, ch 3, 3 dc) in next Shell, ch 7, work Shell in next Shell, ch 7; repeat from ★ 2 times **more**, work Shell in each of next 4 Shells, ch 7 †, work Shell in next Shell, repeat from † to † once; join with slip st to top of beginning ch-3.

Rnd 20: Slip st in next 2 dc and in first sp, work beginning Shell, † ch 4, (sc, work Picot, sc) in center ch of next loop, ch 4, ★ work Shell in each of next 2 ch-3 sps, ch 3, skip next ch-5 sp, sc in next 2 dc, work Picot, sc in next dc, ch 3, work Shell in next ch-3 sp, 3 dc in next ch-3 sp, work Picot, 3 dc in next ch-3 sp, work Shell in next ch-3 sp, ch 3, skip next ch-5 sp, sc in next 2 dc, work Picot, sc in next dc, ch 3, work Shell in each of next 2 ch-3 sps, ch 4, (sc, work Picot, sc) in center ch of next loop, ch 4, work Shell in next Shell, ch 4, (sc, work Picot, sc) in center ch of next loop, ch 4; repeat from ★ 2 times **more**, work Shell in next 4 Shells, ch 4, (sc, work Picot, sc) in center ch of next loop, ch 4 †, work Shell in next Shell, repeat from † to † once; join with slip st to top of beginning ch-3, finish off.

October

Finished Size: Approximately 12″ in diameter

MATERIALS
Bedspread Weight Cotton Thread (size 10),
approximately 110 yards
Steel crochet hook, size 6 (1.50 mm) **or** size needed
for gauge

GAUGE: Rnds 1-4 = 2½″

PATTERN STITCHES
Picot: Ch 3, slip st in stitch just made.

Double Treble Crochet (abbreviated dtr): YO 3 times,
insert hook in stitch indicated, YO and pull up a loop
(5 loops on hook), (YO and draw through 2 loops on
hook) 4 times.

Treble Crochet (abbreviated tr): YO twice, insert hook
in stitch indicated, YO and pull up a loop (4 loops on
hook), (YO and draw through 2 loops on hook) 3 times.

Ch 8, join with slip st to form a ring.

Rnd 1 (Right side)**:** Ch 3, 15 dc in ring; join with slip st
to top of beginning ch-3: 16 sts.

Rnd 2: Ch 5, (dc in next dc, ch 2) around; join with
slip st to third ch of beginning ch-5: 16 ch-2 sps.

Rnd 3: Ch 6, (dc in next dc, ch 3) around; join with
slip st to third ch of beginning ch-6.

Rnd 4: Slip st in first sp, ch 1, 4 sc in same sp,
(2 sc, work Picot, 2 sc) in next ch-3 sp, ★ 4 sc in next
ch-3 sp, (2 sc, work Picot, 2 sc) in next ch-3 sp; repeat
from ★ around; join with slip st to first sc.

Rnd 5: Ch 3, dc in next 3 sc, (ch 10, skip next 4 sc, dc
in next 4 sc) around, ch 5, dtr in top of beginning ch-3
to form last loop: 8 loops.

Rnd 6: Ch 3, 5 dc in same loop, 14 dc in next loop
and in each loop around to first loop, 8 dc in first loop;
join with slip st to top of beginning ch-3.

Rnd 7: Ch 1, sc in same st, (ch 3, skip next dc, sc in
next dc) around, ch 1, hdc in first sc to form last loop.

Rnd 8: Ch 1, sc in same sp, ch 7, skip next ch-3 sp, sc
in next ch-3 sp, ch 7, skip next 2 ch-3 sps, sc in next
ch-3 sp, ★ ch 7, (skip next ch-3 sp, sc in next ch-3 sp,
ch 7) twice, skip next 2 ch-3 sps, sc in next ch-3 sp;
repeat from ★ around, ch 3, tr in first sc to form last
loop: 24 loops.

Rnd 9: Ch 1, sc in same loop, (ch 7, sc in next loop)
around, ch 3, tr in first sc to form last loop.

Rnd 10: Ch 1, sc in same loop, work Picot, (ch 7, sc in
next loop, work Picot) around, ch 3, tr in first sc to form
last loop.

Rnd 11: Ch 3, 3 dc in same loop, (ch 10, 4 dc in next
loop) around, ch 5, dtr in top of beginning ch-3 to form
last loop.

Rnds 12-15: Repeat Rnds 6-9: 72 loops.

Rnd 16: Ch 1, sc in same loop, ch 7, (sc in next loop,
ch 7) around; join with slip st to first sc.

Rnd 17: Slip st in first loop, ch 1, (4 sc, ch 5, 4 sc) in
same loop and in each loop around; join with slip st to
first sc, finish off.

22

November

PATTERN STITCHES

Picot: Ch 3, slip st in stitch just made.

Beginning Shell: Ch 3, (dc, ch 2, 2 dc) in same stitch or space.

Shell: (2 Dc, ch 2, 2 dc) in stitch or space indicated.

Treble Crochet *(abbreviated tr)*: YO twice, insert hook in stitch indicated, YO and pull up a loop (4 loops on hook), (YO and draw through 2 loops on hook) 3 times.

Double Treble Crochet *(abbreviated dtr)*: YO 3 times, insert hook in stitch indicated, YO and pull up a loop (5 loops on hook), (YO and draw through 2 loops on hook) 4 times.

Picot Shell: (2 Dc, ch 5, slip st in fourth ch from hook, ch 2, 2 dc) in space indicated.

Finished Size: Approximately 28" x 14"

MATERIALS

Bedspread Weight Cotton Thread (size 10), approximately 1½ balls (282 yards per ball)
Steel crochet hook, size 6 (1.50 mm) **or** size needed for gauge

GAUGE: Each Motif = 4½"

FIRST MOTIF

Ch 6, join with slip st to form a ring.

Rnd 1 (Right side): Ch 3, dc in ring, work Picot, 2 dc in ring, (ch 3, 2 dc in ring, work Picot, 2 dc in ring) 3 times, ch 1, hdc in top of beginning ch-3 to form last sp: 4 sps.

Note: Loop a short piece of thread around any stitch to mark last round as **right** side.

Rnd 2: Work beginning Shell in same sp, ch 5, (work Shell in next ch-3 sp, ch 5) around; join with slip st to top of beginning ch-3.

Rnd 3: Slip st in next dc and in first ch-2 sp, work beginning Shell, ch 5, (sc, work Picot, sc) in next loop, ch 5, ★ work Shell in next Shell (ch-2 sp), ch 5, (sc, work Picot, sc) in next loop, ch 5; repeat from ★ 2 times **more**; join with slip st to top of beginning ch-3.

Rnd 4: Slip st in next dc and in first ch-2 sp, work beginning Shell, ★ † ch 5, (sc, work Picot, sc) in next loop, ch 7, (sc, work Picot, sc) in next loop, ch 5 †, work Shell in next Shell; repeat from ★ 2 times **more**, then repeat from † to † once; join with slip st to top of beginning ch-3.

Rnd 5: Slip st in next dc and in first ch-2 sp, work beginning Shell, ch 5, skip next loop, 7 dc in next ch-7 loop, ch 5, ★ work Shell in next Shell, ch 5, skip next loop, 7 dc in next ch-7 loop, ch 5; repeat from ★ 2 times **more**; join with slip st to top of beginning ch-3.

Rnd 6: Slip st in next dc and in first ch-2 sp, work beginning Shell, ★ † ch 5, skip next loop, work Shell in next dc, (skip next 2 dc, work Shell in next dc) twice, ch 5 †, work Shell in next Shell; repeat from ★ 2 times **more**, then repeat from † to † once; join with slip st to top of beginning ch-3.

Rnd 7: Slip st in next dc and in first ch-2 sp, ch 3, dc in same sp, ★ † ch 5, slip st in fourth ch from hook, ch 12, slip st in fourth ch from hook, ch 2, 2 dc in same sp, ch 7, (sc, work Picot, sc) in next Shell, [ch 9, (sc, work Picot, sc) in next Shell] twice, ch 7 †, 2 dc in next Shell; repeat from ★ 2 times **more**, then repeat from † to † once; join with slip st to top of beginning ch-3, finish off.

SECOND MOTIF

Work same as First Motif through Rnd 6.

Rnd 7 (Joining rnd): Slip st in next dc and in first ch-2 sp, ch 3, dc in same sp, ch 5, slip st in fourth ch from hook, ch 4, holding **First Motif** with **right** side facing, slip st in center ch of any corner loop on **First Motif**, ch 8, slip st in fourth ch from hook, ch 2, 2 dc in same sp on **Second Motif**, ch 7, (sc, work Picot, sc) in next Shell, ch 4, skip next loop on **First Motif**, slip st in center ch of next loop, ch 4, (sc, work Picot, sc) in next Shell on **Second Motif**, ch 4, slip st in center ch of next loop on **First Motif**, ch 4, (sc, work Picot, sc) in next Shell on **Second Motif**, ch 7, 2 dc in next Shell, ch 5, slip st in fourth ch from hook, ch 4, skip next loop on **First Motif**, slip st in center ch of next loop, ch 8, slip st in fourth ch from hook, ch 2, 2 dc in same sp on **Second Motif**, ★ † ch 7, (sc, work Picot, sc) in next Shell, [ch 9, (sc, work Picot, sc) in next Shell] twice, ch 7 †, 2 dc in next Shell, ch 5, slip st in fourth ch from hook, ch 12, slip st in fourth ch from hook, ch 2, 2 dc in same sp; repeat from ★ once **more**, then repeat from † to † once; join with slip st to top of beginning ch-3, finish off.

ASSEMBLY

Work remaining 8 Motifs, joining 2 strips of 5 Motifs.

Note: When joining corners of three or four Motifs, always join into the same ch as previous joining.

BORDER

Rnd 1: With **right** side facing and long edge toward you, join thread with slip st in center ch of upper right corner loop; ch 19, ★ † skip next ch-7 loop, tr in center ch of next ch-9 loop, ch 9, tr in center ch of next ch-9 loop, ch 14, skip next ch-7 loop, (dtr in joining, ch 14, skip next ch-7 loop, tr in center ch of next ch-9 loop, ch 9, tr in center ch of next ch-9 loop, ch 14, skip next ch-7 loop) across to next corner loop †, (dtr, ch 7, dtr) in center ch of next loop, ch 14; repeat from ★ 2 times **more**, then repeat from † to † once, dtr in same ch as beginning ch-19, ch 3, tr in fifth ch of beginning ch-19 to form last loop.

Rnd 2: Ch 3, 3 dc in side of same st, ★ dc in each ch and in each st across to center ch of next corner loop, (dc, ch 3, dc) in center ch; repeat from ★ 2 times **more**, dc in each ch and in each st across, dc in same ch as beginning ch-3, ch 1, hdc in top of beginning ch-3 to form last sp.

Rnd 3: Work beginning Shell in same st, ★ † ch 3, skip next 4 dc, work Shell in next dc, (ch 1, skip next 4 dc, work Shell in next dc) across to within 4 dc of next of corner ch-3 sp, ch 3 †, work Shell in center ch of corner ch-3 sp; repeat from ★ 2 times **more**, then repeat from † to † once; join with slip st to top of beginning ch-3.

Rnd 4: Slip st in next dc and in first ch-2 sp, work (beginning Shell, ch 2, 2 dc) in same sp, ch 3, work Shell in next Shell, ★ (ch 1, work Shell in next Shell) across to next corner Shell, ch 3, work (Shell, ch 2, 2 dc) in corner Shell, ch 3, work Shell in next Shell; repeat from ★ 2 times **more**, (ch 1, work Shell in next Shell) across, ch 3; join with slip st to top of beginning ch-3.

Rnd 5: Slip st in next dc and in first ch-2 sp, work beginning Shell, work Shell in next ch-2 sp, ch 3, work Shell in next Shell, ★ (ch 1, work Shell in next Shell) across to next corner ch-3 sp, ch 3, skip next ch-3 sp, work Shell in each of next 2 ch-2 sps, ch 3, work Shell in next Shell; repeat from ★ 2 times **more**, (ch 1, work Shell in next Shell) across, ch 3; join with slip st to top of beginning ch-3.

Rnd 6: Slip st in next dc and in first ch-2 sp, work beginning Shell, (ch 3, work Shell in next Shell) twice, ★ (ch 1, work Shell in next Shell) across to next corner ch-3 sp, (ch 3, work Shell in next Shell) 3 times; repeat from ★ 2 times **more**, (ch 1, work Shell in next Shell) across, ch 3; join with slip st to top of beginning ch-3.

Rnd 7: Slip st in next dc and in first ch-2 sp, ch 3, dc in same sp, ch 5, slip st in fourth ch from hook, ch 2, 2 dc in same sp, ★ † (ch 1, work Picot Shell in next sp) twice, ch 3, sc in next ch-3 sp, ch 3, work Picot Shell in next Shell, (ch 1, work Picot Shell in next Shell) across to next corner ch-3 sp, ch 3, sc in next ch-3 sp, ch 3 †, work Picot Shell in next Shell; repeat from ★ 2 times **more**, then repeat from † to † once; join with slip st to top of beginning ch-3, finish off.

December

PATTERN STITCHES

Beginning 3-tr Cluster: Ch 3, ★ YO twice, insert hook in **same** space and pull up a loop, (YO and draw through 2 loops on hook) twice; repeat from ★ once **more**, YO and draw through all 3 loops on hook.

3-tr Cluster: ★ YO twice, insert hook in stitch indicated and pull up a loop, (YO and draw through 2 loops on hook) twice; repeat from ★ 2 times **more**, YO and draw through all 4 loops on hook.

Treble Crochet *(abbreviated tr)*: YO twice, insert hook in stitch indicated, YO and pull up a loop (4 loops on hook), (YO and draw through 2 loops on hook) 3 times.

2-tr Cluster: ★ YO twice, insert hook in stitch or space indicated, YO and pull up a loop, (YO and draw through 2 loops on hook) twice; repeat from ★ once **more**, YO and draw through all 3 loops on hook.

Picot: Ch 4, slip st in third ch from hook, ch 1.

V-St: (Tr, ch 3, tr) in space indicated.

Cluster: YO twice, insert hook in **same** stitch, YO and pull up a loop, (YO and draw through 2 loops on hook) twice, YO twice, skip next space, insert hook in **next** stitch, YO and pull up a loop, (YO and draw through 2 loops on hook) twice, YO and draw all 3 loops on hook.

Finished Size: Approximately 15″ in diameter

MATERIALS

Bedspread Weight Cotton Thread (size 10), approximately 1 ball (282 yards per ball)
Steel crochet hook, size 6 (1.50 mm) **or** size needed for gauge

GAUGE: Rnds 1-4 = 2½″

Ch 8, join with slip st to form a ring.

Rnd 1 (Right side): Ch 1, 12 sc in ring; join with slip st to first sc.

Rnd 2: Ch 1, sc in same sc, (ch 3, sc in next sc) around, ch 1, hdc in first sc to form last sp: 12 ch-3 sps.

Rnd 3: Ch 1, sc in same sp, (ch 5, sc in next ch-3 sp) around, ch 2, dc in first sc to form last loop.

Rnd 4: Work beginning 3-tr Cluster in same st, (ch 7, work 3-tr Cluster in center ch of next loop) around, ch 3, tr in beginning 3-tr Cluster to form last loop: 12 Clusters.

25